SURVIVORS

EXTRAORDINARY TALES FROM THE WILD AND BEYOND

DAVID LONG

Illustrated by Kerry Hyndman

FABER & FABER

For Victoria Ewen

First published in the UK in 2016
First published in the USA in 2017
by Faber and Faber Limited
Bloomsbury House
74–77 Great Russell Street
London WC1B 3DA
This paperback edition first published in 2017

Designed by Faber and Faber
Printed in India

978-0-571-33966-2

10 9

Contents

For as long as people have looked for adventure, some have also found danger, and when it comes to stories of survival few can match the true tales told in this book. Sometimes the individuals know they are taking huge risks, while others are just incredibly unlucky. But in every case these men, women and children have been forced to battle against almost impossible odds – at sea, in the air, and in horrifying situations down on the ground.

As you'll read in the following pages, they needed to find amazing reserves of strength, fortitude and self-belief to come through it all safely. Not everyone emerges unscathed, and quite a few suffer serious injuries, but their stories are exciting, insightful and inspirational – and, however unbelievable, absolutely true.

The girl who fell from the sky (Peru, 1971)

On Christmas Eve, seventeen-year-old Juliane Koepcke was flying high above the South American rainforest when the airliner carrying her and her mother was hit by a violent storm. The previous evening had been prom night at Koepcke's school, but now term was over and they were heading home for the holidays. Home meant the remote Amazonian town of Pucallpa in Peru, where Koepcke's father, Hans-Wilhelm, worked as a biologist. Her mother, Maria, was an ornithologist who studied birds and their behaviour. Sharing her parents' passion for science and nature, Koepcke planned to follow their example by studying biology at university.

On board the four-engined Lockheed Electra aeroplane she could hear other passengers complaining because their flight had been delayed by nearly seven hours. But they were airborne now and Koepcke was happy to be on holiday and looking forward to seeing her father. From her window seat she noticed storm clouds in the distance, but she loved flying and had no reason to feel afraid.

She began to feel anxious as the Electra dipped suddenly and entered a massive, rain-dark cloud

Her mother felt less relaxed about the storm. Never quite believing that something metal could rival the birds she studied, Maria didn't like flying at the best of times. Now she began to feel anxious as the Electra dipped suddenly and entered a massive, rain-dark cloud. Before long the plane was being buffeted about by the air currents, and after a few minutes even Koepcke began to feel that something wasn't quite right.

Bags and other pieces of luggage started to fall from the overhead racks and drinks tipped into passengers' laps. Soon Christmas presents and parcels began bouncing around the cabin as the aircraft was pitched up and down by the turbulence.

Through her window Koepcke could see flashes of lightning around the aircraft. With the storm obviously closing in she too began to feel scared. Above the sound of the propellers several passengers could be heard crying as she reached across for her mother's hand.

The violent pitching continued like this for nearly ten minutes, throwing the aircraft this way and that. Gripping her mother's hand more tightly now, Koepcke looked out of the window and saw that one of the engines was glowing brightly. Her mother also noticed this and very quietly said, 'That is the end. It's all over.' These were the last words Koepcke ever heard her say.

Moments later the cabin was plunged into darkness, and the Electra went into a steep nosedive. Koepcke couldn't see anything in the pitch black, and could hear nothing but the roar of the engines. Then, just as suddenly, everything went silent. With a shock the teenager realised she was somehow outside the aeroplane, still strapped in her seat but tumbling over and over and over. With nothing around her but the rush of cold air, she was plummeting down towards the jungle.

With a shock the teenager realised she was somehow outside the aeroplane

Coming out of the clouds she momentarily glimpsed the tops of the trees spinning up to meet her like a patch of giant broccoli. It was petrifying, but she must have passed out immediately because the next thing she remembered was waking up the following morning. It was Christmas Day. She was still strapped into her seat, but it was now wedged firmly into the ground.

Forty minutes after taking off, the aircraft had apparently been struck by lightning, one deadly bolt causing a fuel tank to explode and rip off the right wing. As the fuselage began to disintegrate around her, Koepcke had been thrown clear of the airborne wreckage and then fell more than two miles down into the jungle below.

Despite the trauma of this experience, she realised at once what had happened. Looking up at the trees she knew she had survived an air disaster, probably because her seat had broken the fall as she crashed through the dense foliage.

> Looking up at the trees she knew she had survived an air disaster

Unsurprisingly, the seventeen-year-old was in considerable pain and feeling dizzy. She had broken her collarbone, damaged a ligament in one knee, and sustained deep cuts and bruises as she hit the ground. Her left eye was also swollen shut, but she could still walk and knew she had to start finding a way to safety.

Koepcke had learned enough about the jungle from her parents to know it wasn't as dangerous as people like to think. Travelling on foot, it was important to keep a cool head and not do anything foolish, but she had no idea where she was, or where any of the other passengers had come down. She had also lost a shoe and her glasses, which complicated things as she was very short-sighted. Nor was she dressed for a jungle trek, with only a light cotton summer dress to protect her from the hordes of biting, stinging insects that were buzzing all around her.

The first thing to establish was if anyone else was nearby, especially her mother, but when Koepcke called out there was no response except the chatter of startled animals. Some time later she was thrilled to hear an aircraft circling overhead. Presumably the crew were looking for survivors, but since she couldn't see the plane through the thick canopy of trees she quickly guessed they couldn't see her either. This realisation made her feel utterly alone.

For a while the Koepckes had lived in a remote scientific research station, and Hans-Wilhelm had taught his daughter some useful survival tips. For example, he told her that **Walking through shallow water can be safer than walking on land** walking through shallow water can be safer than walking on land – snakes and other venomous creatures are hard to spot on the ground and may attack if anyone steps too near them. Koepcke also knew that jungle settlements tend to be built along rivers, so if she stayed near water she would stand a better chance of meeting someone and finding help.

Until this happened, however, her situation looked desperate. She had nothing to eat except a small bag of sweets, and she had no idea how far she might have to walk to reach safety. Soon dozens of insects were dropping onto her skin and climbing into her hair, and with the sun up the rain forest was unbearably hot. It was also very wet because torrential storms like the one that had brought down the Electra continued on and off throughout the day.

Having failed to find signs of anyone nearby Koepcke started to walk, and when she came to a small stream she decided to follow it. It was lucky that there was plenty of water to drink, but the rainy season meant there was no ripe fruit on the trees, and from her parents' jungle training she knew that eating anything else would be too risky.

At nightfall the temperature dropped dramatically, and with her sleeveless dress wet through Koepcke felt terribly cold. She also felt very lonely as well as frightened. Unable to sleep, she sat shivering as she listened

to the startling sounds of the rainforest at night. **It didn't take long**
The following morning she continued slowly **before the little bag**
along the course of the stream. It didn't take long **of sweets was empty**
before the little bag of sweets was empty, and
when her watch stopped she rapidly lost track of time.

After a couple of days she heard the sound of a king vulture somewhere nearby. From her mother Koepcke knew these huge carnivores tend to land only where there is lots of food around. Knowing they eat only dead animals, she had to consider the gruesome possibility that the bird was looking for bodies from the plane.

To her horror her fears were proved correct shortly afterwards when she stumbled upon a bank of seats from the aircraft. It was partly buried in the undergrowth and Koepcke could see three bodies still strapped in place. For a moment she thought one of them might be her mother, but then she noticed nail varnish on the toes, which Maria never wore. In fact, Koepcke never did find any more survivors during her time in the jungle; she later learned that of the ninety-one people on board the Electra she was the only one left alive.

For several days she continued her journey downstream, alternately walking and swimming. This made her progress very slow, and swimming led to serious burns from the sun beating down on her back and arms. Together with her other injuries this caused her more and more pain, while a lack of sleep and the effort needed to keep moving only added to her exhaustion. She was also alarmed to find that the insect bites were becoming infected and that live maggots were now burrowing under her skin.

After a week Koepcke realised that she could no longer hear aircraft

above, meaning that the authorities must have stopped looking for survivors. This scared her but also made her very angry, knowing they had given up even though she was in the jungle below still fighting for her life. She began to despair, but on the ninth day, to her astonishment and delight, she found an old, broken-down boat on a stretch of riverbank where she'd been resting.

Her first thought was to take the boat, but she didn't want to be accused of stealing. Instead she looked around and noticed a path running up the bank and into the trees. Climbing the path took all her strength as she was so tired and hungry, but at the top she found a small shack. Inside it was an outboard motor and a can of fuel, which reminded her of a trick her father used to cure the family dog of worms.

Climbing the path took all her strength as she was so tired and hungry, but at the top she found a small shack

Pouring petrol onto her wounds ought to kill the maggots, or at least get them off her skin. Koepcke knew the stinging would be excruciating but it had to be worth a try. After dousing one arm in the flammable liquid she counted no fewer than forty maggots as they dropped out of her wounds and onto the ground. The effort left her even more exhausted, and wrapping herself in a tarpaulin from the shack she quickly fell asleep.

Waking the following day Koepcke didn't feel much better and decided to stay in the shelter a bit longer because she was too tired to move. Outside she could hear another rainstorm beginning, but later, as the rain died away, she thought she could hear voices approaching the shack. Struggling to her feet and pulling open the door she was overjoyed to see three forestry workers. The men were astonished, and she quickly explained about the crash and how she had spent the last ten days alone in the forest.

The men offered her some food, but after so long without anything except water she was unable to eat. They quickly decided to take her downriver in their canoe. After seven hours on the water she was flown to a hospital, and then reunited with her father in Pucallpa. Happily, Koepcke went on to make a full recovery, although for years afterwards she was haunted by nightmares about her ordeal and the loss of her mother and the other passengers. Juliane Koepcke never lost her love of biology, however, and after qualifying in Germany she has returned to Peru many times to visit the rainforest and study its wildlife.

Douglas Mawson
The man who came home alone
(Antarctica, 1912)

A time known as the heroic age of polar exploration saw several explorers racing to be the first to reach the South Pole. However, other explorers were more interested in research than glory. With a team of two dozen scientists, the Australian geologist Douglas Mawson set out on a dangerous mission to study the vast frozen continent of Antarctica.

The men established a base camp on the coast, a cramped wooden hut that quickly became snowbound. Setting out from here Mawson and two of his companions began to explore inland. Lieutenant Belgrave Ninnis was in charge of the dogs used to pull supplies and equipment. Xavier Mertz, a champion skier from Switzerland, came with the skills of an experienced mountaineer. Keen to examine the geology of the region, the three planned to trek more than 1,200 miles across the ice, but after six weeks they'd managed to cover little more than a quarter of this distance.

In what experts agree is the windiest place on Earth, the weather was far worse than Mawson had anticipated. Wind speeds in Antarctica can hit nearly two hundred miles an hour and roaring windstorms frequently last for weeks on end. When this happens it is impossible to stand upright, and with visibility as low as three feet the men often had to resort to crawling forward on their hands and knees.

At night they pitched their tents against the howling wind, and each morning a mask of ice and snow would form on their faces. Bizarrely, this offered them some protection from the ferocity of the weather. The trio managed to make good progress to begin with, but as their pace slowed it was becoming clear that they were heading into danger.

Each morning a mask of ice and snow would form on their faces

The three men had successfully traversed two huge glaciers and were 311 miles from base when Ninnis suddenly disappeared. The ground he was crossing looked like solid ice but it was actually just a fragile crust of frozen snow. Beneath this lay a crevasse so deep it might as well have been bottomless, and when the crisp snow gave way under his weight Ninnis fell into the void with his sledge and six of the twelve dogs.

Beneath this lay a crevasse so deep it might as well have been bottomless

There was no hope of rescuing Ninnis or the animals, since even crawling to the edge of the crevasse meant risking further tragedy. Mawson and Mertz estimated that Ninnis must have fallen at least 150 feet, which was beyond the reach of the ropes they carried on the remaining sledge and made it impossible to save him, even if he'd survived.

Besides the shock of losing their friend, the two men now faced potential disaster. Their tent and waterproof clothing had disappeared into the crevasse, along with most of the food. All the food for the dogs was lost as well, and vital tools such as the pickaxe and shovel. Mawson and Mertz still had a stove, fuel and sleeping bags, but barely enough food for ten days.

Their only option was to turn back, but with a return journey of several weeks their situation looked extremely bleak. By retracing their steps the two men could at least recover some damaged equipment they'd abandoned a couple of days earlier. Some of it might prove useful now that they were in such danger, but there was still the problem of where to find food.

Mawson felt there were two courses open to them. The first was to take the route back along the coast, where they might supplement their rations by killing seals for meat. This was a much longer route, however, and the terrain would be harder and more dangerous. Alternatively pushing further south would get them get back to the hut more quickly but without the possibility of seal meat they would have to kill some of the dogs. This was a horrible decision to have to make but the only way to feed themselves and the remaining animals.

It was a grim task but they shot the weakest dog first

It was a grim task but they shot the weakest dog first. Before setting out for the hut they fried some of the meat for themselves and gave the raw remainder to the hungry pack. The flavour was on the whole quite good, Mertz thought, except for the liver, which was too stringy to chew properly.

Mawson suggested that from then on they ought to trek at night: the colder temperatures would make their progress over the frozen snow faster than during the day. When not travelling they would rest in a temporary shelter which Mertz rigged up from a tent cover and ski poles.

On long expeditions it's often only the thought of a break and a hot meal that keeps polar explorers pushing on, but with supplies severely rationed both men now tried desperately not to think about how hungry they were. As the days wore on it was obvious the dogs were also weakening from the lack of food. Two more were shot, and once again the men kept the best bits for themselves and threw the rest to the remaining three dogs.

Before long all the dogs were despatched in this way. Forced to haul everything themselves, the men were beginning to feel ill as well as worn out. Mawson noted in his diary that Mertz was 'off colour', but in fact both of them were suffering badly. Besides stomach pains and diarrhoea, Mawson and Mertz noticed their skin was beginning to peel off in great chunks. Neither knew it but this was a classic symptom of vitamin A poisoning, a side effect of eating dog liver, which is toxic to humans.

Mertz was sickening much faster than Mawson, and was soon having regular fits and finding it difficult to even talk. After rapidly weakening he died peacefully at two o'clock one morning, leaving Mawson alone and more than a hundred miles from safety. Worse still, he knew that if he failed to reach the hut within the next seven days the ferocity of the returning Antarctic winter would mean the ship that was scheduled to take the scientists home would not be able to come back for him for another eight months.

Depressed and badly frostbitten, Mawson buried his friend and rested for a day, during which time he inspected his feet. He was horrified to find the soles literally falling off in two blood-soaked pieces, another result of eating dog liver. After bandaging his feet tightly he pulled on six pairs of socks to hold everything in place. Then, in excruciating pain, he resumed his long, lonely walk.

More than once the ground gave way beneath him and, like Ninnis, Mawson tumbled down into a deep crevasse. He was only saved by the rope attached to the sledge, which remained wedged above him. Fearing he would never make it back to the hut he tried desperately to find the strength and willpower to haul himself up the rope. For a while he just hung there until, from somewhere within himself, he found what he needed and began to climb. The effort nearly killed him, and once back on the surface he could do no more than lie on the frozen ground while drifting in and out of consciousness.

He was only saved by the rope attached to the sledge, which remained wedged above him

Alone in the endless blizzard, simple things such as erecting the shelter now took hours to complete, and with no dogs to pull the sledge Mawson's rate of progress was slowing by the day. Aware that he might never reach the hut, he contemplated giving up. Several times he thought he should just eat what little food remained and then wait to die. Fortunately, he resisted the temptation. Desperately hungry but hoping for the best, he decided to push on as fast as he could.

Desperately hungry but hoping for the best, he decided to push on as fast as he could

Three weeks after Mertz's death Mawson was still many miles from base, and the weather was getting worse. The sheet ice underfoot made walking harder than ever, but he struggled on. Soon he was down to his last few ounces of raisins and chocolate, and had only a few scraps of dog meat. Somehow he managed to cover fourteen miles without a break, and then another six, after a fitful few hours spent dozing in his mouldering sleeping bag.

By 8 February Mawson had been walking alone for a full month. He was only a couple of miles short of his destination when, by some miracle, the blizzard suddenly lifted. In the clear and calm conditions he could see dark shapes ahead – were they rocks or men? As they moved forward to meet him, he realised that his agonising walk back from death was finally at an end.

The first words he'd heard in weeks said everything about his physical condition. 'My God,' one of his scientist colleagues asked, 'which one are you?' The exhausted Mawson was in such poor shape after his ordeal that his teammates could no longer recognise him. All they could do was cook him some hot food and hope that over time he would begin to recover.

It turned out that the rescue ship had left just hours earlier but, incredibly, six very brave men had volunteered to stay behind in case any of the expedition team made it back to the camp. Now one of them had. It would take many months for another vessel to reach them and a year before they were home, but Douglas Mawson was on the slow road to recovery.

HANS PETER STRELCZYK AND GÜNTER WETZEL

The friends who crossed the border by balloon (Germany, 1979)

For more than forty years, from 1949–90, political differences meant that Germany was split in half and had two separate governments. Germans living in the Communist-controlled eastern sector were forbidden from crossing into the West, and a heavily armed border with attack dogs, guard towers and minefields prevented them even visiting friends and family living on the other side.

Many refused to accept defeat and often showed considerable ingenuity in thinking up new ways to flee their half of the country

Nevertheless, there were many attempts to cross the border, and several hundred citizens died trying to reach the West in the belief that life there would be better. Some were shot dead by border guards, others were killed in the minefields. Still, many refused to accept defeat and often showed considerable ingenuity in thinking up new ways to flee their half of the country.

One of the most daring plans was hatched by former aircraft mechanic Hans Peter Strelczyk and his friend Günter Wetzel, a bricklayer. Keen to smuggle their wives and four young children out of East Germany, they realised it was too dangerous to escape by land. Instead, after seeing a television documentary about the early days of manned flight, they decided to try and fly over the border. Their idea was to cross at such a height that the guards below would not be able to spot them and shoot them down.

Having worked in the aircraft industry Strelczyk knew it would be impossible for them to get their hands on an aeroplane. However, he was confident they could construct a simple flying machine, and the pair decided to design and build their own hot-air balloon.

In Communist countries, even if you have the money, it's often impossible to buy certain things. The East German secret police, known as the Stasi, would have been very suspicious if they'd heard of someone attempting to buy a hot-air balloon or the equipment needed to make one. Because of this

Wetzel and Strelczyk had to be crafty. The balloon would have to be made at home and in secret, using things the men and their families could obtain without anyone realising they were planning to escape.

They worked out that four ordinary household gas cylinders could be bolted together to fuel the burner needed to heat the air in the balloon. It would also be relatively easy to make a basket to hang beneath it for the passengers. But both men knew that lifting eight people would be difficult, even though four were children. It would require a really big balloon, which meant lots and lots of suitable fabric.

They decided to buy the fabric in modest amounts, and visited many different shops where they would purchase only small quantities each time. To further disguise what they were doing they pretended they were using the fabric for camping or sailing. This seemed the best way to avoid arousing suspicion, but it meant a lot of travelling and a great deal of hard work to stitch the small pieces together. Over several months the men and their wives, Petra and Doris, spent many hours working on an ancient sewing machine making a balloon more than sixty-five feet in diameter.

None of them had made anything like this before, and it took a while to find the best kind of material. Some turned out to be too thin and the air leaked out as the balloon was inflated. Others were more airtight but much heavier, meaning the balloon would strain to get airborne.

With eight lives at stake it was essential that they got everything right

With eight lives at stake it was essential that they got everything right, and so Wetzel devised a simple machine to test how airtight each type of material was. Using an old vacuum cleaner to suck air through the fabric, he measured the amount of air that leaked through, and by weighing the individual fabrics he determined which type was the best.

Despite this meticulous approach the first two attempts failed. The first balloon was badly damaged while it was being packed away in a hurry after the families thought someone was spying on them. The second also ran into problems because so much fuel was used to inflate it with hot air that there wasn't enough left in the tanks to fly across the border.

The men were also worried that their secret had been discovered when a story appeared in one of the local newspapers saying that the Stasi were looking for anyone who might have information about an escape attempt by balloon. When they read the article the men and their wives realised they would either have to move faster or abandon their escape plan altogether. After discussing it among themselves they decided to have a third go as soon as possible, this time using a balloon made from even lighter fabric.

The men and their wives realised they would either have to move faster or abandon their escape plan altogether

The results from Wetzel's experiments suggested the ideal solution was a combination of umbrella material, tent nylon and taffeta, a lightweight cloth used for wedding dresses and ball gowns. Once again every effort was made to buy sufficient quantities without arousing suspicion. At weekends Strelczyk and the two women would drive out to shops many miles from where they lived. Wetzel and one of the older children stayed at home stitching the balloon.

The amount of material they managed to buy would have covered seven tennis courts. Even so, bed sheets had to be used to complete the balloon when several of the shops ran out of supplies. The families now had to work very fast to ensure the balloon was completed before the end of the summer: the wet weather would make it impossible to fly safely, and the Stasi might come looking for them.

It was very hard work but by mid-September everything was ready, and the weather looked sufficiently clear for a third attempt. There was no time left to test the new balloon but, hoping for success, the Strelczyks and Wetzels drove out to a hill between the towns of Oberlemnitz and Heinersdorf. Not too far from the border and hidden in a forest clearing, they had decided this spot would be an advantageous place to launch the balloon. The plan was to lift off at around midnight, travelling in the dark to avoid being seen.

It took a while to search the area to make sure they were not being watched. Then, working as quickly and as quietly as they could, the would-be escapers began to assemble their equipment. The basket was secured to the ground using four short ropes and the gas cylinders were fixed in place. Once this was done it took just five minutes to inflate the huge balloon, which was very noisy and made everyone worry that somebody might investigate what they were up to.

The bright flare from the gas burners was another potential giveaway. Praying nobody would spot the glow, the two families clambered into the basket and prepared to launch. As the air in the balloon warmed up they slowly began to lift off the ground – their plan was working! Wetzel and Strelczyk cut the four ropes and the balloon rose swiftly into the cool night air.

Praying nobody would spot the glow, the two families clambered into the basket and prepared to launch

In the light of the burners they could see a tear in the fabric, but otherwise everything seemed to be going smoothly. Within minutes they were nearly two thousand feet above the ground, and caught in a strong wind they began to travel along at speed. The ride must have been exhilarating but also frightening – after all, this was an untested, homemade balloon, piloted by amateurs with no formal training and no professional navigational skills.

To begin with it was impossible to tell how fast they were travelling. At this height it was also very cold, and as it was the middle of the night there were no lights below to help them work out where they were. With the balloon spinning round and round, they quickly lost their bearings and couldn't be sure the wind was carrying them in the right direction.

It was very cold, and there were no lights below to help them work out where they were

Before long, however, they saw searchlights in the distance, which presumably meant they were nearing the border. Powerful beams of light repeatedly swept across the night sky, but the families were confident the balloon was flying too high to be spotted.

A few minutes later the burners began to splutter and die. Several desperate attempts were made to relight the jets before it became apparent that the gas had run out. The balloon could only go down, but fortunately its descent was fairly gentle. After a while everyone on board could make out the tops of trees in the gloom, and then with a sudden crash the basket ploughed into the ground. In a muddy field in the middle of nowhere their flight to freedom was over.

At this point no one had any idea where they had come down.

The families had to face the possibility that they had not managed to cross the border before running out of gas. They knew the border was close, but was it in front of them or behind? More tired than afraid, and freezing cold, the eight passengers began to walk away from the balloon. They realised that they might encounter border guards with machine guns rather than a friendly West German farmer.

After crossing several fields they came to a farm building. The children hid with their mothers while the men went to investigate. On the way one of them spotted a sign on a pylon, which read Überlandwerk, a name neither man recognised from home. Next, in a deserted barn, they found gleaming modern farm machinery. This was much newer and far superior to the old tractors used in East Germany, and for the first time the men dared to hope that their plan had succeeded.

As they stood there wondering what to do next a car appeared and a couple of uniformed men got out. Wetzel and Strelczyk were relieved when they didn't recognise the uniforms. They must be West German police uniforms, they thought, and not those of the hated Stasi. Just to be sure, they asked whether they were now in West Germany. 'Of course you are,' replied one of the policemen. 'Where else would you be?'

The Strelczyks and the Wetzels were free

It took a while to answer this question, and to explain how they had got there, but the important thing was that the Strelczyks and the Wetzels were free. Naturally, there was a lot of interest from the media about how the two families had made their escape, but after a while it quietened down and they were able to build new lives for themselves in the west of Germany.

TAMI OLDHAM
The woman who sailed into a hurricane (Pacific Ocean, 1983)

Keen and experienced mariners, twenty-three-year-old Tami Oldham and her fiancé Richard Sharp were sailing a luxury yacht from Tahiti in the South Pacific to the American port of San Diego. The voyage should have taken a month, and with good weather forecast the pair were looking forward to enjoying some excellent sailing and a great adventure. Before long, however, the trip of a lifetime turned into a fight for survival when their boat was hit by a deadly category-4 hurricane.

In 160-mile-per-hour winds the forty-four-foot *Hazana* was soon being battered by giant rolling waves, while a solid wall of salt-laden spray reduced visibility almost to zero. On her way down to the cabin Oldham was knocked unconscious by the impact of an especially violent wave, while on deck Sharp struggled to stay in control of the boat. Eventually it capsized, and when she came to there was no sign of her companion. *Hazana* had righted itself but was now adrift and badly damaged. The main mast had gone and a quick inspection revealed that the electrical circuits and engine had been disabled by three feet of water flooding the hull.

She was at least fifteen hundred miles from Hawaii, the nearest land mass

Oldham estimated that she was at least fifteen hundred miles from Hawaii, the nearest land mass. She was badly injured, losing blood from a head wound, and in shock at the discovery that the love of her life had apparently been washed overboard. She knew he would have been tethered to the boat by a safety line, but in the buffeting of the storm the line must have snapped.

Looking at her watch she thought she must have been unconscious for nearly three hours. In fact she was a whole day out. After sustaining the painful blow to her head she'd spent almost twenty-seven hours lying motionless down below.

Considering her situation, the temptation to give in was overwhelming, and initially Oldham came close to surrendering in the face of what looked like an insurmountable challenge. For a couple of days, stunned by the death of her fiancé, she did nothing and ate nothing. Only slowly did she realise that she had to snap out of it. She couldn't just give up and wait to die.

Calling for help was not an option Calling for help was not an option. The yacht's radio, sophisticated electronic navigation system and the emergency position-indicating equipment had all been fatally damaged in the storm. On the plus side, the *Hazana* still had plenty of food and water on board, and Oldham was a talented and knowledgeable sailor. She and Sharp had logged more than fifty thousand miles on the water – equivalent to sailing twice around the equator – and so she knew she had the skills needed to reach dry land.

She also knew how to plot a course from the positions of the sun and stars, which she could do using her watch and a traditional navigational device called a sextant. Somehow the rudder had survived the impact of the hurricane, which meant the boat could still be steered, and Oldham was confident she could improvise a mast and a new sail using bits and pieces salvaged from the wreckage. However, this proved difficult because of the extensive damage to the boat: as well as capsizing, the *Hazana* had at one point flipped end over end.

The greatest danger was that she was adrift somewhere in the middle of the Pacific, by far the largest ocean on Earth. Over sixty million square miles and covering approximately one third of the planet's entire surface, the sheer size of the Pacific meant simply drifting was too risky. There was no hope that someone would find her. Instead she would have to sail to safety.

She knew that her most urgent task was to pump out the water from the hull before getting rid of everything that had been smashed during the storm. To move around the boat safely it was important to clear the deck of the broken spars and wrecked sails, and to tidy away the ropes. These included the remains of Sharp's lifeline, torn loose by the force of the hurricane.

The sensible thing was to tackle these jobs one at a time, to have a plan and to remain focused on working through that plan. Keeping going can seem impossible when facing huge struggles alone, but like other people in life-threatening situations Oldham tuned into a voice in her head – a sort of inner spirit, perhaps – which was encouraging her to persevere. Listening to the voice, she knew that to have any chance of surviving she first had to decide to be a survivor.

To have any chance of surviving she first had to decide to be a survivor

She managed to rig up a makeshift mainsail using one of the smaller sails, which had been safely stowed below during the storm. A couple of days' practice with the sextant enabled her to figure out where she was. From the yacht's charts and using the ocean currents, Oldham was reasonably sure she could plot a course that would take her towards Hawaii.

The small temporary sail meant the *Hazana* would be much slower than before. Without Sharp, and sailing solo, she would also have to work round the clock just to keep the boat travelling in the right direction – it had to be kept on course at night as well as during the day. Realising that the voyage to safety would probably take many weeks, she knew she faced a punishing routine: without anyone to share the burden there were no opportunities for her to take time off to sleep properly or to regain her strength.

Deeply depressed and suffering from the monotony of this routine, the highlight of her day was using the sextant to figure out her location, the mental exercise being a relief from the physical grind. By marking the time when the sun is at its highest point, and then again as it dips down to the horizon, a good sailor can work out their position very precisely. Using these calculations Oldham was able to reassure herself that she was indeed heading for Hawaii, and also measure how far she had travelled since the previous day.

> **The highlight of her day was using the sextant to figure out her location, the mental exercise being a relief from the physical grind**

Weather conditions fluctuate wildly in mid-ocean, but luckily there was no repeat of the hurricane. On good days Oldham reckoned she could travel as much as sixty miles; at other times the *Hazana* was becalmed and barely moved at all. With only the small sail to catch the wind, the boat's progress was fairly slow, and with such a huge distance to cover it was nearly six weeks before Oldham came in sight of dry land and saw another vessel.

It was on the forty-first day that her luck finally changed. Exhausted and emaciated, she was at last spotted by a Japanese research vessel called the *Hokusei Maru*, which took the *Hazana* in tow. Shortly afterwards the two boats were met by US Coastguard personnel, who escorted them into Hilo harbour on Hawaii's Big Island.

Oldham was safe, but by this time she had lost nearly a third of her bodyweight. She was also suffering from severe shock as a result of her ordeal, but having battled heartbreak, fear and depression, she knew she had conquered the mighty Pacific. Managing to cross a daunting 1,500 miles of open ocean, she had shown an incredible combination of skill, knowledge and sheer determination – and done it by listening to a voice that told her she had to choose to stay alive.

ROGER CHAPMAN AND
ROGER MALLINSON
The men who shared a sandwich on the seabed (Atlantic Ocean, 1973)

Approximately 150 miles off the coast of Ireland, the submersible *Pisces III* was engaged in an operation to lay underwater telephone cables from Europe to North America. Beginning early one Wednesday morning, the minisub's two pilots, Roger Chapman and Roger Mallinson, expected to spend a normal eight-hour shift working nearly 1,640 feet below the surface of the Atlantic Ocean. Slowly traversing the seabed, Chapman and Mallinson were part of the team responsible for setting up pumps and jets to clear a path through the mud and sand for the cables. Working at such a depth meant the task was potentially dangerous, but the men were experienced and had done this kind of thing many times before.

Diving down to the seabed took about forty minutes. Once at the bottom the work required absolute concentration on the part of both crewmembers. At such a depth it is always dark, and swirling debris adds to the poor visibility. The sub's cramped interior didn't help either – a roughly spherical space barely six feet in diameter. Both men had to spend the long hours kneeling and bent over double with their heads close to their knees.

At such a depth it is always dark, and swirling debris adds to the poor visibility

They took turns piloting the sub and controlling a giant mechanical hand called a manipulator. This is used to position equipment outside while the sub moves slowly along the seabed at around half a mile an hour.

Mallinson had been hard at work long before the shift began. Much of the previous day and night was spent repairing the manipulator, which had been damaged during an earlier dive. As a qualified engineer he was familiar with all the intricacies of *Pisces III*. During his pre-dive preparation he also replaced the sub's oxygen tank with a full one, which contained more than enough gas for the next eight-hour shift.

His colleague's background was quite different. As an ex-Royal Navy submariner Chapman was used to much larger vessels than this one, and when out on patrol he would have spent far longer periods submerged than his present job required.

Their shift passed without incident. As a safety measure, everything that happened during the eight hours was recorded using the sub's on-board video; equally important, a device called a lithium-hydroxide fan soaked up the dangerous carbon dioxide the men breathed out. Now the shift was over *Pisces III* was bobbing about on the surface. Once a line was attached to it the men would be hauled back onto the support vessel.

This part of the operation was always noisy and uncomfortable, with lots of crashing and banging as their crewmates fixed the line to the submersible. But this time something went badly wrong. Inside their cramped quarters Mallinson and Chapman suddenly found themselves thrown upside down as they hurtled back towards the ocean floor when the sub lost buoyancy.

This time something went badly wrong

Catastrophically, a rear part of the sub had flooded when a hatch was opened on the surface. This made it nearly a tonne heavier. They were now sinking exceptionally fast. Both men realised nothing could be done to stop them sinking, but from their training and experience they knew they must somehow slow the descent, otherwise they would be crushed by the impact of the submersible hitting the seabed.

Equipment was flying around the cabin, with bits and pieces breaking loose as *Pisces III* plummeted into the depths. Moving as quickly as they could, Mallinson and Chapman switched off everything electrical. In complete darkness they managed to disconnect a four-hundred-pound lead weight, which under normal circumstances helped the sub descend to the seafloor at the start of each shift.

Everything was now happening at breakneck speed, the motor screaming and pressure gauges and other instruments whirling round and round as the sub spiralled out of control. Grabbing seat cushions to give their bodies some protection, and stuffing bits of cloth into their mouths to prevent them biting off their tongues, the pair steeled themselves as best they could for the inevitable crash.

The pair steeled themselves as best they could for the inevitable crash

After plunging down into the dark for an agonising thirty seconds the impact when the sub hit the bottom was brutal. Later it was established that they must have crashed at around forty miles per hour, but miraculously neither of them was hurt. It was immediately obvious, however, that the damage to the sub meant they would not be able to resurface under their own power. Having come to rest a terrifying 1,640 feet beneath the surface, the two men were in the dark and on their own.

Flashing the beam of a torch they surveyed the chaos around them. To their surprise they were still able to communicate with the surface. A quick telephone call to the support ship established that both men were all right, and that a rescue attempt would begin immediately. However, everyone involved knew that the challenge was daunting and that no one had ever been rescued from such a depth before.

Chapman and Mallinson must have been relieved that thanks to the replacement of the tank the previous day they had plenty of oxygen. A full tank contains enough for seventy-two hours (equivalent to three days and nights), of which they had used just eight during their shift. There was almost nothing to eat or drink, except for a single cheese and chutney sandwich and a can of lemonade. Luckily, neither of the men felt particularly hungry.

There was almost nothing to eat or drink, except for a single cheese and chutney sandwich and a can of lemonade

It was extremely cold this far down, but knowing that people need far more oxygen when they're active the pair decided the best thing would be to find a comfortable position and remain as still as possible. It was also important to get as high up as they could since foul air, being heavier than fresh, would soon begin to collect at the bottom of the cabin. From now on neither spoke, another way of preserving the oxygen, but they would squeeze hands occasionally as a way of reassuring each other that everything was OK.

Above them a major rescue mission was underway. To begin with the support ship could do little aside from monitoring the situation, but a sister submersible, *Pisces II*, was ordered to return to its nearest port and join the operation. While the Royal Air Force flew one of its Nimrod aircraft overhead, HMS *Hecate* of the Royal Navy was also racing to the scene. It was to be joined by the Canadian Coast Guard's *John Cabot*, and *Curv III*, a highly specialised US Navy submersible used to salvage atomic weapons from deep underwater.

Curv III was based in California, nearly six thousand miles away, but remarkably it arrived on site within twenty-four hours. The name is short for 'Cable-controlled Undersea Recovery Vehicle', making it the ideal tool for the job. Even so, especially now that bad weather was closing in, no one

was in any doubt that rescuing the sub from such a deep location would be exceptionally difficult.

By the time *Curv III* was ready for action the two men had been trapped for thirty-six hours, which meant half their oxygen supply was already used up. To conserve power, the men were using the lithium-hydroxide fan sparingly instead of every forty minutes, which was the standard recommendation. This meant the air quality in the sub was declining rapidly and making it harder to breathe.

The air quality in the sub was declining rapidly and making it harder to breathe

The polluted air made both men drowsy and lethargic. Neither of them wanted to touch the sandwich or the lemonade. They were also worrying about their families: Chapman had only just got married, and the Mallinsons had four young children. During the long wait a personal message from Queen Elizabeth briefly lifted their spirits, though it turned out to be not from the Queen but from the crew of the *Queen Elizabeth II*, the famous cruise liner.

On Friday, more than two days after the men had begun their dive, the first attempt was made to lift them off the seabed. Unfortunately, it failed when a submersible damaged its rope before reaching the required depth. A second sub had run out of power by the time it located the two men and had to resurface. Then, just as *Curv III* was preparing to dive, an electrical fault was discovered and it couldn't be launched.

Chapman and Mallinson were kept informed of what was going on, but by midnight their hopes were fading fast. Their seventy-two hours were now officially up. Added to this, there was no more lithium hydroxide left to run the fan even occasionally, and there were now more broken vehicles on the surface than working ones. Using the telephone they could sometimes hear the happy sound of dolphins swimming around above them, but their situation was looking grim.

Work continued overnight to get *Curv III* running again, and it was Saturday morning before first one line and then a second were successfully attached to the men's sub. Only then did they decide to share the cheese and chutney sandwich and the lemonade, although by this time neither of them quite believed the rescue would work.

Slowly they began to rise from the seabed, but something felt very wrong. *Pisces III* was moving around violently, and twice the lifting stopped, which caused both men unimaginable anguish. On the first attempt *Curv III* became tangled in the lines and had to be freed. Then, just one hundred feet from the surface, there was another wait while divers attached heavier lines to ensure the sub didn't sink again.

Slowly they began to rise from the seabed, but something felt very wrong

In all it took two and a half hours to reach the surface, and even then the ordeal wasn't over. At first it was thought the two men might have been killed by the speed of the ascent, and when it took a further thirty minutes to wrench open the damaged hatch there were serious concerns about their lack of oxygen. In fact, when it was finally opened there was just twelve minutes' supply left in the tank. This was such a slender margin for survival, and quite astonishing as they had by then been depending on the seventy-two-hour tank for a total of eight-four hours and thirty minutes.

After so long cooped up in such cramped quarters both men found it impossible to climb out unaided. Decades later Roger Chapman says he still finds it hard to get into a lift as he doesn't like the up and down motion. Despite everything, both men continued to work in the same industry, each commending the other for keeping a cool head in truly desperate circumstances.

ARON RALSTON

The canyoneer who cut off his own arm (Colorado, U.S.A. 2003)

In the wide, open country of rural North America the sport of canyoneering involves hiking through wild, rocky landscapes, as well as jumping, climbing, scrambling, abseiling and even swimming. Whatever it takes, in other words, to traverse the most challenging terrain the country has to offer.

Aron Ralston became a mechanical engineer after leaving university, but as a keen outdoorsman he soon abandoned this career to spend more time in the mountains. In particular, he had a dream to climb what Americans call the 'fourteeners', a series of nearly sixty mountain peaks in the state of Colorado, each rising to more than fourteen thousand feet. Ralston planned to do it climbing alone, and in the depths of winter.

One Saturday in April 2003 he was enjoying quite a different challenge, one that should have been a lot easier. He was spending the day travelling on foot through a remote part of Utah's beautiful Canyonlands National Park. Not for the first time he was out on his own, but that morning he made **He made the simple but potentially fatal error of not telling anyone where he was going** the simple but potentially fatal error of not telling anyone where he was going.

Ralston figured he would be out for no more than eight hours, but his troubles began when he attempted to climb down into a particularly narrow slot canyon. As the name suggests, this is a rock crevice much deeper than it is wide. Usually this sort of feature forms as the result of erosion, when water from a creek or stream carves its way down through the bedrock.

The process takes many thousands of years but the results can be spectacular, and Utah boasts more slot canyons than anywhere else in the world. The most impressive are wild and rocky ravines, often a hundred feet deep but no more than three and a half feet from one side to the other. Not surprisingly, they're hugely popular among hikers and mountaineers, both for their beauty and for the excitement they offer the serious climber.

Tackling the one known as Blue John Canyon, Ralston was slowly descending by rope when he inadvertently dislodged a huge sandstone boulder. It had been wedged between the canyon walls but under the force of gravity it now suddenly shifted downwards. It didn't have far to fall but when it came to rest it was crushing his right hand. Worse, the boulder had pinned his arm against the unforgiving face of the rock wall and he was unable to move.

The pain was intense and Ralston cried out instinctively, but in such a remote place there was no point in calling for help. In his agony and fury he shouted and swore repeatedly, but even in his traumatised state he would have known that the chances of his voice carrying up and out of the deep, narrow canyon were zero. In fact, he very quickly realised he might die there, trapped in a sheer-sided rocky abyss. Blue John was miles from anywhere and no one even knew the lone hiker was missing.

As far as supplies were concerned, at least he had a little water and a couple of burritos. He knew they had to be rationed, but even if he was lucky enough to be discovered it might not be any time soon. After four days there was no sign of help. He was still trapped and the water was all gone. No help came the following day either, and by Thursday he had no food left.

Despite the agonising injury to his hand he made strenuous efforts to move the boulder, but it wouldn't budge, not even slightly. Weighing around eight hundred pounds, or the same as several grown men, it was impossible to shift no matter how hard Ralston tried pushing with

He tried chipping away at the boulder using a multi-tool he carried with him

his feet and knees or using a kind of improvised rope cradle. Later he tried chipping away at the boulder using a multi-tool he carried with him, but after many hours it had barely made any impression on the diamond-hard surface.

If he couldn't move the boulder to free his arm, then he would have to remove his arm to free the rest of his body

The rock was stuck fast, and so was Ralston. Now he realised that he needed to consider a much more drastic solution. The reasoning was simple enough: if he couldn't move the boulder to free his arm, then he would have to remove his arm to free the rest of his body. It had been done before: ten years previously a fisherman in Colorado had cut off his own leg after it became trapped in a rockfall; and a bulldozer driver had done the same thing with a small penknife after being pinned down by a tree.

Incredibly, both men had survived, and done so despite the shock and considerable loss of blood. But a trained surgeon using the best equipment would still think twice before undertaking any kind of self-surgery – and Ralston was a former engineer, not a doctor. All he had was the multi-tool, which was blunted by his efforts to attack the surface of the boulder, and the knowledge that after five days stuck under the huge rock he had no other choice but to try.

Because of the damage to his multi-tool Ralston realised he would have to use the smaller of its two blades. It was barely two inches in length and far from ideal for the job. Also Ralston was right-handed so using his left hand to cut would be even harder. Nevertheless, with the kind of courage that comes only in the worst situations, he began to cut into his own flesh.

At the same time he had to staunch the flow of blood by tying a tight band called a tourniquet around his upper arm – all of this with only one hand and regardless of the enormous pain.

Even more excruciating than cutting through his flesh, however, were the nerves and tendons. The latter, the strong sinews which bind together our bones, were severed using the tool's built-in pliers, but by far the worst part of the operation came when Ralston hit a nerve. Even touching a nerve can cause electrifying pain, but actually severing one sent a bolt of lightning or super-heated fire shooting up to his shoulder.

Ralston was free – of his arm and of the mighty, immovable boulder

In all, the operation took around an hour, each moment pure agony, until suddenly the impossible was done: Ralston was free – of his arm and of the mighty, immovable boulder. It was, he later said, the happiest moment of his life. He knew he was in desperately urgent need of medical attention, and still a long way from home, but mentally he felt in good shape.

The full realisation of what he had just done seems to have given him a great sense of personal power, that and knowing he was not going to die alone in Blue John Canyon. Somehow, with his one remaining arm, he managed to lower himself around sixty-five feet to the bottom of the narrow rock fissure, and after taking a long and overdue drink from a filthy, fetid pool of water he began the next part of his journey home.

Now good fortune was on his side. Members of a search and rescue team were out looking for him, having found his truck several miles away, but after so long they expected to find a corpse. Ralston could certainly see that he was losing blood at a very dangerous rate, but before his battered, dehydrated body gave out for good, he was lucky enough to encounter a young family.

They had come thousands of miles from the Netherlands to hike the canyon, and what little food and drinking water they carried they gladly handed over to the distraught American. In the blistering heat the mother and son ran ahead to get help while the father remained behind with the injured man. Two hours later and close to collapse Ralston at last heard the sound of an approaching helicopter.

After many months in hospital and a series of painstaking surgeries, his recovery was remarkable

After many months in hospital and a series of painstaking surgeries, his recovery was remarkable. As park rangers laboured to remove the dangerous boulder – in the end it took thirteen men, a winch and a powerful hydraulic jack – Aron Ralston stuck by his determination to conquer the 'fourteeners'. He did it too, in the harsh cold of winter, and became one of only three people to have accomplished it while climbing alone.

Poon Lim
The man who sucked blood from a shark (Atlantic Ocean, 1942)

During the Second World War twenty-five-year-old Poon Lim worked as a ship's steward on board SS *Benlomond*. The vessel was carrying cargo between South Africa and South America when it was attacked by a

German submarine hundreds of miles off the coast of Brazil.

To the commander of the German submarine *U-172* the old ship must have looked like an easy target. During the course of five or six patrols his crew had destroyed more than two dozen Allied vessels. *Benlomond*, travelling alone, only lightly armed and very slow, took just two minutes and a couple of torpedoes to join their deadly tally.

It sank so quickly that fifty-three sailors and gunners perished almost immediately. Poon Lim was the only crewmember to escape with his life, having grabbed a lifejacket before jumping into the sea. Unable to swim very well, the Chinese-born Lim spent a couple of hours floating helplessly in the water before finding an eight-foot-square life raft among the drifting wreckage. Frightened and exhausted, he managed to clamber aboard.

It sank so quickly that fifty-three sailors and gunners perished almost immediately

We now know the attack took place approximately 750 miles from the mouth of the mighty River Amazon. Lim would not have known this at the time, as he was employed in the kitchens rather than as a sailor with any knowledge of navigation. All he knew was that the little life raft could not be sailed or steered like a proper boat. His only hope was that he would see another ship before too long, or float close enough to the coast to shout for help.

He was fit and practically minded, and knew he could make good use of the emergency supplies which, together with some rope, were stored in the raft. These included several tins of dry biscuits and some chocolate, six gallons of fresh water and a big bag of sugar lumps. There were also emergency flares, a couple of smoke grenades and a torch, any one of which could be used to send a signal if he spotted a ship near enough to rescue him.

Lim calculated that he might survive for about a month if he rationed the water and allowed himself two biscuits in the morning and another two in the evening. Of course, this was assuming he didn't run into bad weather that might cause the raft to capsize. He also needed to drift towards the coast, where someone might see him.

Within the first few days he saw two other vessels on the horizon. One was another enemy sub, and the other a cargo freighter like the *Benlomond*. He could see men on the deck of the freighter and signalled frantically, but apparently no one saw him as it steamed on past him. On another occasion Lim thought he'd been spotted by the pilot of a low-flying US Navy patrol plane, but no boat was sent to pick him up.

As his supplies began to dwindle Lim formulated a plan to stay alive

His disappointment helped him realise very quickly that he was now on his own. He knew that if he were to stand any chance of surviving it would depend entirely on his own skills and his own resourcefulness. As his supplies began to dwindle Lim formulated a plan to stay alive.

With no shelter from the sun his skin was burning badly, which he could do nothing to prevent. Weight loss was another problem, but determined to stay fit he started to exercise by paddling in the sea around the raft. Before jumping in he used a piece of rope to tie himself to the raft to stop it drifting away from him. Soon he was swimming nearly every day, the only exceptions were when he saw sharks in the vicinity.

Avoiding dehydration was always his first priority: people can survive for many days without food but not very long without water. Using the canvas lining from his lifejacket Lim rigged up a simple device for catching rainwater. He knew that the supplies would not last much longer, and that he had to get some food fast.

People can survive for many days without food but not very long without water

To do this he used a piece of wire from inside the torch, which he painstakingly fashioned into a crude fishhook. And by unravelling some of the rope securing the emergency supplies to the raft he made a length of fishing line.

One of the last pieces of dry biscuit provided the bait, and when Lim hoiked out his first fish he was able to gut it using a crude but effective blade made from a section of the biscuit tin. Some of the fish he caught he ate raw, and the rest he set aside to use as bait.

He was soon catching fish regularly, but most of them were small and after eating them he was still very hungry. The raft often attracted the attention of seagulls and Lim began to wonder whether it would be possible to catch a bird to eat using the rotting fish as bait. He decided to give this a go, and after placing some smelly strips of fish on the edge of the raft he lay as still as he could. Eventually one of the birds came to investigate the smell, and as it landed on the raft Lim shot out his hand and grabbed the bird by the neck.

A fight ensued, during which the bird proved to be surprisingly strong. As it lashed out with its beak, Lim's hands and arms were cut several times, but in the end he managed to subdue the bird and kill it using his homemade knife. Once again the hard-won prize had to be eaten raw, but the success of the method encouraged him to try for even larger prey. **Over the next** **couple of days** **he hatched a** **bold plan to** **catch a shark** Over the next couple of days he hatched a bold plan to catch a shark. From time to time the creatures circled the raft and he knew if he could catch one it would provide enough food for several days.

He thought half a seagull would be the perfect bait but realised he would need a much bigger hook than the little piece of wire he'd been using to catch fish. Fortunately, by working it backwards and forwards, he was able to prise a large nail out of the raft's planking. He bashed it into shape using one of his shoes and the empty water container, which he filled with seawater to increase its weight. From start to finish reshaping the metal nail took a couple of days, but eventually it was ready and Lim settled down to wait for a likely victim to appear.

To his relief the first shark to spot the bait was less than seven feet in length. Cautiously approaching the raft it suddenly lunged at the dead bird and swallowed the hook, which pulled the line taut. Lim was ready and sprang into action, grabbing the poor shark by the tail, pulling it backwards and then wrestling it onto the raft.

Unable to breathe air, sharks can't survive long out of water, but sensing danger this one wasn't going to give up easily. Lim knew he would have to fight hard to keep it on the raft. Protecting his hands by wrapping them in canvas from the lifejacket, he held the shark down with one hand and used the other to hit it repeatedly with the water container.

Despite the blows, the shark thrashed around with growing desperation. Furiously snapping its teeth-lined jaws it flexed its strong body again and again in an attempt to get off the raft and back into the sea. It was an exhausting duel for both, but gradually the shark began to tire. Unable to breathe, its thrashing weakened and eventually it lay still. The great battle was over and Lim had won his prize.

Using his tin blade again he cut the shark open and sliced off its fins. There had been no rainfall for several days and his water supply was now dangerously low: drinking the blood provided him with life-saving nourishment. Later, after the fins had dried in the sun, Lim was delighted to find that they reminded him of the shark's fin soup he used to enjoy back home on Hainan Island off China's southern coast.

> **There had been no rainfall for several days and his water supply was now dangerously low**

Ever since the shipwreck he'd been counting the number of days he'd been lost at sea. As the weeks wore on, however, it became too depressing and he began counting full moons instead. They happened only every twenty-eight days, but as the total grew, lonely Lim began to consider the possibility that he might never find land and never be rescued.

From his observation of the moon he knew that well over four months had passed. Then, at last, he noticed that the sea was gradually changing colour. The deep blue of the mid-ocean was slowly giving way to the pale green of coastal waters. Lim also saw birds flying high overhead – land birds rather than the seagulls he'd been eating. There was seaweed drifting around the raft too, suggesting he was at last in shallower water.

Finally, on his hundred and thirty-third day afloat, he spotted a white sail far away on the horizon. It was the first boat he'd seen in many months. Jumping up and down, he waved his shirt frantically to attract the attention of anyone on deck.

For a while nothing happened, and then to his great joy he realised that the sail was slowly changing direction. Before long the small boat was heading towards his raft, and squinting into the sun he saw three people on board. They were fishermen, Brazilians who spoke only Portuguese. Even without a shared language they knew that this bony fellow was in trouble and needed their assistance. After helping him on board they gave him fresh water and some dried beans. Soon the little boat was heading for the coast and away from the raft that had been Lim's home – his whole world – for nearly four and a half months.

In fact, Lim had survived alone on his raft for longer than anyone else before or since. His skin was badly blistered and having lost over twenty pounds he looked more like a skeleton than a steward. But now Poon Lim was safe and, after a four-week spell in a Brazilian hospital, he was finally homeward bound.

Lim had survived alone on his raft for longer than anyone else before or since

ERNEST SHACKLETON
The commander who saved his crew
(Antarctica, 1914)

In August 1914, as part of the Imperial Trans-Antarctic Expedition, a ship left Britain under the leadership of the sailor and polar explorer Sir Ernest Shackleton. His intention on reaching Antarctica was to cross the continent on foot, a journey of more than 1,800 miles through the ice-bound wilderness, a truly epic feat which had never before been accomplished.

Shackleton had been to Antarctica twice already, and on his second trip had managed to travel further south than any man before him. Since then, the Norwegian Roald Amundsen had become the first to reach the South Pole, making Shackleton keener than ever to reclaim glory for Britain. Members of the public were just as enthusiastic, and more than five thousand people attempted to join his crew.

Shackleton's ship *Endurance* left London the same day that war on Germany was declared. On board were twenty-eight scientists and sailors, plus the ship's mascot, a tiger-striped cat called Mrs Chippy. They were accompanied by more than sixty dogs, trained to pull the sledges containing supplies when six of the men, handpicked by their leader, would eventually set out across the ice on wooden skis.

The voyage south took several months, and it was December before the *Endurance* reached the cold waters around Antarctica. In an area known as the Weddell Sea the crew had to navigate a safe route through great sheets of floating ice that bumped noisily against the ship. **Great sheets of floating ice bumped noisily against the ship** These ice floes pose a constant danger in this part of the world, even during what passes for summer in the southern hemisphere.

Progress became agonisingly slow, and very soon the *Endurance* ground to a halt as the ice formed a solid barrier around its wooden hull. It was the first of many such incidents, and over the coming weeks entire days were spent drifting at the mercy of ferocious winds.

At other times the crew found themselves stuck fast in the ice and going nowhere. Eventually land was sighted in the far distance, but with the ice thickening around the ship there was no possibility of reaching it.

Before long the *Endurance* was stuck solid and the men faced the awful realisation that it might be months before the ice melted and freed them to continue their journey. Occasionally a passing iceberg provided temporary shelter from the wind, but as the weather worsened Shackleton began to fear for their safety. A failed attempt to free the ship by using shovels, saws and pickaxes convinced him that it was time to take decisive action.

As the weather worsened Shackleton began to fear for their safety

With the darkness of winter closing in there was no question of abandoning the ship: it provided their only refuge. The dogs were taken off board, however, and housed in makeshift ice shelters called 'dogloos'. This made a bit more room on board for the men, but it offered precious little in the way of comfort. A radio aerial was rigged up, though it quickly became apparent that the ship's location was far too remote either to send or receive messages.

This meant the men were now completely cut off from the world. Facing a long, cold wait for the ice to melt, Shackleton worked hard to keep everyone mentally and physically fit. He instituted a programme of exercise for the men and training for the dogs, and even organised the occasional race to keep things interesting. The men put on short plays to entertain themselves, and everyone was encouraged to take walks out on the ice when weather conditions permitted.

It was August by the time the ice finally began to melt and release its grip on the ship, a full year since the men had left London. Disaster struck almost immediately, however, when a build-up of ice under the ship caused it to lean perilously to one side. Terrifyingly, with temperatures as low as minus 25°C, massive blocks of ice were now being slammed against the ship by the wind pressure and sea currents.

The danger was obvious and eventually the *Endurance* could take no more. Crushed by the onslaught of the ice, her immense timbers began to bend and crack. One crewmember likened the sound to fireworks or big guns, and as water began to pour into the hull an immediate evacuation was ordered.

As many supplies as could be carried were hastily pulled from the ship, along with three small lifeboats. A temporary camp was established on the ice, and for as long as the ruined ship stayed afloat every effort was made to grab anything else on board that might be useful.

With the ship all but lost, Shackleton knew the expedition had to be abandoned. His patriotic dream of glory now became a desperate fight for survival. The team attempted a march across the ice to safety, but it took them three days to cover fewer than two miles, and eventually they turned back. By the time the *Endurance* finally sank the decision was taken to sit tight and camp out on a large ice floe, in the hope that its gradual drift would take them closer to land.

His patriotic dream of glory now became a desperate fight for survival

To conserve what little food they had, but to the horror of some of the team, the weaker dogs were shot, along with poor Mrs Chippy. Small

pieces of timber wrenched from the ship were used to make replacement boots for the men who needed them. An order was issued that any passing seal should be shot. This would supplement their meagre diet, while the fat from the blubber could be used as fuel for the stoves.

Drifting on the ice in sub-zero temperatures the crew of the *Endurance* occasionally came within sight of land but, as before, they were never close enough to reach it. Worse still, the ice was now starting to melt, and as their own floe began to break up Shackleton hastened his men into the three small lifeboats. As commander his new objective was to reach one of several tiny, inhospitable islands lying within a couple of hundred miles of their position. None were inhabited, and many remained unvisited from one year to the next, but they seemed a better prospect than simply drifting.

After some discussion they chose Elephant Island, a bleak, ice-covered rock, which if nothing else would give Shackleton time to consider his next move. To reach it would take at least another week. They spent the days and nights dodging icebergs, soaked through with saltwater, their meagre rations soon gone. Amazingly, they made it, and when all twenty-eight men scrambled ashore it was the first time in nearly a year and a half that any of them had set foot on dry land.

Shackleton hastened his men into the three small lifeboats

They were still far from safe, however. Elephant Island was uninhabited and unimaginably remote. Hundreds of miles from civilisation, its only visitors were the infrequent whaling ships which occasionally sheltered there during the Southern Ocean's famously ferocious storms. It also lacked any plant or animal life, meaning that once again the crew would have to survive on seal meat and the occasional penguin.

Fortunately, Shackleton had a plan. More than nine hundred miles away, across the dangerous, slate-grey sea, lay the island of South Georgia. It was larger than Elephant Island, but equally desolate. However, there was a whaling station on the far side, and Shackleton believed that if he could reach it he might be able to find a ship and return to rescue his men.

It was a fearsome journey for a small lifeboat, even a foolhardy one, but it was the only chance Shackleton had of saving his men's lives. Selecting five crewmembers to accompany him, he began to plot a course. To make it more waterproof a mixture of paint and seal blood was daubed on the strongest of the three boats, and a new mast was made using wood from the other two. Four weeks' rations were placed aboard, the calculation being that if it took longer than a month to reach the whaling station then everyone was doomed anyway.

It was the only chance Shackleton had of saving his men's lives

As the boat set off the sea was beginning to freeze again, and another storm was visible on the horizon. Within a day they were clear of the worst of the pack ice, but in rolling waves and a ferocious gale the little boat was tossed about like a feather. Desperate to stay afloat, the men worked in two shifts of three: one steering, one manning the sails and the third bailing out the water rushing over the sides. Attempts at navigation relied on the fleeting appearances of the sun and was often no better than guesswork, but on the fifteenth day seagulls were spotted, then floating seaweed, and finally – land.

Even then it took more than twenty-four hours to find somewhere to beach the boat. Once on land, Shackleton quickly realised they were on the opposite side of the island to the whaling station. Unfortunately, after so long on the storm-tossed ocean the lifeboat was now too decrepit to risk a journey around the treacherous rocky coast. Besides, three of the six men were too exhausted to walk. The only option was for the other three to try and cross the island on foot.

This would involve a hike of at least thirty miles without maps or even the most basic equipment. The trio would also have to climb a mountain range and cross several glaciers – a formidable challenge for even the fittest and freshest adventurer.

Shackleton and his two companions were neither fit nor fresh, but they knew they had no choice. Climbing, clambering and eventually staggering – non-stop, in order to stay awake – they arrived at the whaling station thirty-six hours later. Their faces blackened by frostbite, exposure and the soot from months huddled over seal-blubber fires, one of the three admitted they looked like 'a terrible trio of scarecrows'. Shackleton, their famous leader, was nevertheless immediately recognised by the whalers, and within hours a boat was sent to recover the three men waiting on the other side of the island.

Shackleton and his two companions were neither fit nor fresh, but they knew they had no choice

With the Great War in progress it took a while longer before a larger ship could be found to rescue the remaining twenty-two men on Elephant Island. Despite this delay, they too were saved. Shackleton had failed in his attempt to cross Antarctica on foot, but in the worst possible circumstances he managed to bring his entire expedition party home alive.

HUGH GLASS
The trapper who grappled with a grizzly (Missouri River, U.S.A. 1823)

American Hugh Glass was a famous nineteenth-century fur trapper and adventurer. He was a legendary figure, and many people believe he spent several years as a pirate before embarking on a hard new life out in the wilderness.

When he was about forty years old Glass decided to join an expedition heading up the Missouri River. With a group of around a dozen experienced frontiersmen he planned to hunt, trap and kill animals for their skins. In the nineteenth century this was still an important industry, and in the wide, open spaces of Montana and North and South Dakota it was possible to make a good living this way. The work was exhausting and dangerous, however, and life in the wilderness was brutal.

Tall and powerfully built, Glass had done this kind of work before and knew the risks. But even the most experienced trapper can make a mistake. While out on his own scouting for food he accidentally surprised an American brown bear and her cubs.

He accidentally surprised an American brown bear and her cubs

Known as grizzlies, these top predators grow to an immense size. With a distinctive hump between its shoulders, an adult male can weigh as much as a small family car and stand at nearly ten foot tall when on its hind legs. Females are slightly smaller but just as fierce. Indeed, a female may react even more ferociously than a male bear if she feels her young are in danger.

This particular grizzly was certainly quick off the mark. Before Glass could aim his rifle the bear knocked him off his feet, swept him up into the air, and then with massive force hurled him down onto the rocks.

Dazed but fully conscious, he quickly got to his feet. Unable to see his gun anywhere he pulled out his hunting knife and tried to fight the beast off. Stabbing repeatedly as the bear lunged at him, Glass dodged and ducked to avoid her four-inch claws. Somehow, he eventually managed to wrestle the huge animal to the ground, but by this time he had several deep, bloody gashes on his back and arms. The worst of them had gone right through to the bone.

Almost crushed beneath the dying bear's body, Glass's injuries were horrific. It took only moments for his friends to come running when they heard him screaming, but by the time they reached

Somehow, he eventually managed to wrestle the huge animal to the ground

him he was unconscious and bleeding profusely from several wounds. No one thought he stood even the slightest chance of recovering, not after they saw how much blood had soaked through his tattered clothes and into the ground.

By this stage in the expedition the men were hundreds of miles from anywhere Glass might have received proper medical treatment. He was also far too seriously injured to be moved, but the leader, Major Andrew Henry, knew that no man deserved to be left to die alone.

When he asked for volunteers to stay behind with the dying man two of the trappers raised their hands. For a cash bonus, teenager Jim Bridger agreed to stay, along with an older man called John Fitzgerald. The plan was for them to give Glass a decent burial when he died and then rejoin the main group further along the trail. When their colleagues left shortly afterwards, Bridger and Fitzgerald skinned the bear so they could use its pelt to keep Glass covered.

It seems likely they also dug a grave at this point, in order to move on as soon as Glass was dead. But the following morning he was still alive. His breathing was now even shallower, and encrusted in dried blood he looked worse than ever. But the two men stuck by their duty, although both knew that for each extra day they stayed the expedition force would have moved further and further away.

What happened next has never been entirely clear. Some reports say the two men waited a few days and then left Glass, possibly because they feared coming under attack from local Native Americans known as the Arikaras. In defence of their territory, the Arikaras had certainly killed trappers in the past, but whatever the reason, Bridger and Fitzgerald fled – and their companion was definitely still alive when they left him.

Perhaps assuming he wouldn't last much longer, the men took some of his kit. This included his knife, rifle and some food and other supplies that would have been useful out on the trail.

It's impossible to say how long it took Glass to regain consciousness. When he awoke, maybe hours later, maybe days, he was lying in the shallow grave and wrapped in the bearskin. He was alone with nothing except the shreds of the clothes he'd been wearing when he surprised the bear. His state of mind can only be guessed at, but once he realised he was hundreds of miles from safety, seriously injured and completely unarmed in deeply hostile territory he must have been petrified.

When he awoke, he was lying in the shallow grave and wrapped in the bearskin

Untreated for several days, his wounds were beginning to turn septic. He also had a broken leg, and although he wouldn't have known it, no one was coming to rescue him. We know this because after rejoining the expedition Bridger and Fitzgerald were quick to say they had buried a dead man rather than admitting the truth that they had abandoned a living one.

Good with his hands and resourceful in a crisis, Glass was able to reset his broken leg using a length of branch as a crude splint. His lacerated back was more of a problem, but he had an ingenious if gruesome idea. Finding maggots on a mouldering tree trunk, he knew they liked to eat rotting meat. Pressing his raw back against the trunk was unbelievably painful, but he knew that if he could transfer the maggots onto his body they would clean his wounds. By eating his torn, dead flesh they would prevent him getting blood poisoning, which would have killed him.

Good with his hands and resourceful in a crisis, Glass was able to reset his broken leg

Hoping that he might find food and water along the way, Glass decided to head for a place called Fort Kiowa, a French fur-trading post nearly two hundred miles away. His broken leg and other injuries meant he was unable to walk; indeed, initially he couldn't even crawl. Instead, he had to pull himself along the rough, rock-strewn ground as best he could.

His progress was agonising and painfully slow, and he was forced to take frequent breaks when exhaustion and fever took hold. He would sleep where he lay, on one occasion waking up hours later to find another huge grizzly towering over him, though it's possible this was only a nightmare.

For days and then weeks he ate little except berries and roots, anything he found on the ground that looked like it might contain nourishment. Occasionally he was able to steal eggs from low-lying nests, and then later, having regained some of his strength, he managed to drive off a small pack of wolves that had killed a young bison. Without a knife or flints to make a fire he ate only what could be torn from the bones. He snapped some of the

thinner bones in half to suck out the juices, and though the raw meat was tough and bloody it gave him the energy he needed to keep going.

By his own account, his motivation at this time was the thought of revenge. His memories of the ordeal were hazy and confused, but he just couldn't understand why the other members of the expedition had left him for dead. Whatever the reason, to him it felt like treachery – and he wanted his knife and rifle back.

By his own account, his motivation at this time was the thought of revenge

After nearly two months he was still less than halfway to Fort Kiowa, but his wounds were healing by the time he reached the Cheyenne River. Using branches pulled from trees and woven together he made a crude raft, and knowing the Cheyenne flowed into the Missouri he planned to drift downstream towards the fort. To his great relief the fast-moving current meant he travelled far more swiftly than he had done for many weeks. His desire for revenge grew as he neared his destination.

His arrival at the fort surprised everyone, especially once he recounted his tale of fighting a grizzly and winning, and then managing to survive alone in the wilderness for so long. His recovery took a while longer, but once he was fully fit again he set out to find the men who had left him for dead. At this stage Glass thought he might murder them, on the grounds that they had, in effect, tried to kill him by leaving him without the means to survive.

When he tracked down Bridger, however, he realised he couldn't do it. The boy was young, and if he'd thought the Arikaras were about to attack it was only natural that he would run away. In the end Glass didn't dare kill Fitzgerald either, knowing that if he did he would probably hang for it. Murder is still murder, after all, even for a man who fought a grizzly and then crawled back from the dead.

Mauro Prosperi
The desert runner who drank his own wee (Sahara, 1994)

Completing a marathon is challenging for even the fittest athlete, but the modern ultramarathon is far harder. As well as being much longer than the twenty-six miles of a normal marathon race, they take place in some of the most inhospitable locations on Earth.

Such events can involve climbing high mountain passes thousands of feet above sea level or hiking across glaciers. Others incorporate long-distance swimming and cycling stages, as well as running, skiing and even canoeing. For nearly thirty years the toughest and most extreme is the Marathon des Sables, or Marathon of the Sands, and Prosperi decided to tackle it.

Completing the 156-mile course takes the best athletes nearly a week, and as the name suggests it's run through the Sahara Desert, one of the hottest places in the world. To make it even harder the runners must carry their own food and clothing in backpacks. The temperature in this part of Morocco can reach as high as 58°C during the day, and it drops sharply at night-time, when runners sleep under the stars.

Drinking water is available only from checkpoints along the route. Throughout the event the competitors face many dangers, including deadly snakes, venomous scorpions and enormous camel spiders – up to six inches in diameter and able to run at more than ten miles an hour, they also have a ferocious bite.

The competitors face many dangers, including deadly snakes, poisonous scorpions and enormous camel spiders

Even without the risk of being bitten or stung, the Sahara is a punishing environment. As well as scorching heat and exhaustion from running up to fifty miles in a day, visibility can be cut to only a few inches by the blinding sandstorms that blow up without warning.

It was one of these sandstorms that nearly finished off Prosperi in 1994. In March of that year he lined up with 133 other runners. The Sicilian policeman was a highly experienced competitor and had completed several ultramarathons, as well as making it into the Italian Olympic squad.

This was his first desert event. He ran hard, and by the fourth day was lying in seventh place. Having covered twenty miles that morning he was in reasonably good shape too, although one foot was becoming badly blistered. (Blistering can seriously injure runners, and at least one competitor was flown home for emergency skin grafts.) Prosperi was confident he could still run hard, and after collecting his water ration he set off on the next gruelling stage of the race.

Shortly after lunchtime a strong wind appeared out of nowhere. It rapidly increased in intensity and Prosperi found himself in the middle of a fierce sandstorm. Desert storms like this can be hard to imagine for anyone who has never seen one. Within seconds ground and sky merge into one, and the air is thick with tiny razor-sharp particles of sand. They seem to pierce the skin and, finding their way into the eyes, mouth and ears, the pain can be severe. Meanwhile, in the soupy darkness visibility is cut almost to zero.

The air is thick with tiny razor-sharp particles of sand

Anyone who has experienced a sandstorm knows that it's best to stay where they are until it dies down. However, Prosperi was concerned about becoming buried in the sand, and didn't want to lose his leading position when the storm was over. He felt it would be safer to keep moving, but when the wind eventually dropped and visibility improved he realised straightaway that he was lost.

The storm had lasted more than six hours and many tonnes of displaced sand obscured the course Prosperi was expecting to follow. He knew there was no chance of guessing which way to run, so he reached into his backpack for a distress flare. Runners were required to carry these with them, and by firing one into the still air he could alert the race organisers and let them know where he was.

The flare was fired, but no help came. Unfortunately Prosperi had strayed so far off the marathon course during the storm that no one even saw the flare. The organisers knew he was missing and had sent out a search party, but they had no idea where to look. **In a desert that covered more than four million square miles he was on his own.**

Within hours his water bottle was empty, and he took to urinating in it to give him a source of liquid, should he need it later. He knew enough about desert survival to travel only in the early morning and evening, when the air was relatively cool but there was still enough light to see. But he also knew that even if he could find shade from the midday heat he was facing a horrible death from dehydration.

How far he managed to walk is hard to say, but on his third day alone Prosperi stumbled upon a long-abandoned religious shrine. Inside it was cramped and dark, and as his eyes became accustomed to the gloom he spotted a colony of bats roosting. He killed several of them and then drank their blood. It must have tasted awful and offered little in the way of refreshment, but it was better than nothing. Prosperi realised by now that if things continued like this he would not survive very long.

He reasoned that if he stayed inside the shrine he would eventually be found. He stuck a small Italian flag on the roof, hoping it would attract the attention of anyone who came looking for him, though he accepted that he might be dead by the time they spotted the flag. At

least his family would know what had happened and would have a body to bury.

Like everyone who takes part in these events, he knew that dying of thirst was a particularly ghastly death, and he thought hard about killing himself before this happened. He had a pocketknife in his backpack, and after writing a farewell note to his wife and family he decided to use it to cut his wrists. Knowing he would bleed to death, he tried to get into a comfortable position and then waited to die.

To his surprise, he woke up early the next morning. Tired but alive, he looked down at his wrists and saw that there was hardly any bleeding. Possibly because he was so dehydrated his blood had clotted instead of flowing freely. This chance **The previous day he had wanted to die, but now he was determined to live** survival gave him renewed hope. The previous day he had wanted to die, but now he was determined to live, and to see his three children again. Nomads and other people survive in the Sahara, he reasoned, so why shouldn't he?

His near brush with death also renewed his confidence in his strength and abilities. For the next few days he trekked slowly towards the misty mountain range he could see about twenty miles away.

He had nothing left in his backpack to eat on the journey, and nothing to drink except tiny amounts of dew he collected each morning, and the urine stored in his water bottle. No one would suggest drinking it, but things were desperate and Prosperi felt he had no choice.

Over the next few days he was lucky enough to trap small lizards for food, and each night he buried himself in the sand to insulate himself from the cold desert air.

Somehow he kept this up for nine days before finally encountering a group of Tuareg nomads. By now he was

He kept this up for nine days before finally encountering a group of Tuareg nomads

more than 150 miles off course from the marathon, and more than two days drive from the nearest hospital. Having strayed over the border into Algeria, he was now carried by camel to a military base. Initially the soldiers thought he might be a spy, but once this misunderstanding was cleared up they treated him well and arranged transport to take him out of the desert.

Prosperi survived, if only just. Having been close to collapse, it would take him almost two years to recover, after which he was desperate to return to the Sahara. The great desert had nearly killed Mauro Prosperi but it had bewitched him too. Perhaps understandably, for a couple of years the organisers flatly refused his applications to re-enter the race. Then, on the third occasion, they relented. After several unsuccessful attempts he finished thirteenth in 2002.

SUE RUFF AND BRUCE NELSON

The couple who were blasted by a volcano (Washington State, U.S.A. 1980)

Sue Ruff and Bruce Nelson were camping with friends on the mossy north bank of Washington State's Green River. At around eight-thirty in the morning the group of six were happily toasting marshmallows for breakfast. Their plan was to do some fishing in a quiet spot about twelve miles north of a volcano called Mount St Helens.

The volcano is more than eight thousand feet high but Ruff and Nelson were so far away that they couldn't even see its snow-capped peak. Had they known it was about to erupt they might reasonably have assumed they would be safe, but within seconds whole forests for nearly thirty miles around were flattened by the blast. Along with scores of other hikers and loggers they were suddenly in great danger.

We now know that the catastrophic eruption was the deadliest in American history, and by far the most destructive. Two hundred and fifty homes were destroyed almost immediately, together with many bridges and hundreds of miles of road and railway.

The impact triggered a powerful earthquake and, as a column of smoke and ash rose a dozen miles or more into the air, water from melting glaciers on the volcano began to pour down creating the largest mudslide ever recorded. Stretching more than fifty miles, an avalanche of rock and soil careered down the mountainside at an estimated speed of 150 miles an hour. Everything in its path was swept away and buried.

An avalanche of rock and soil careered down the mountainside

The noise was horrifying, one witness later likening it to the sound of several passenger jets flying through the trees. As a vast cloud of burning ash descended on Nelson and Ruff the area around them was plunged into sudden darkness. Unable to see where they were going, the pair stumbled then tripped and fell into a deep hole. They were in shock and disoriented, but crouching below ground they were at least protected from the great cloud of heat swirling around above them.

It took a few minutes for things to calm down, but when they climbed out of the hole they found themselves in the middle of what looked like a lunar wasteland. Aside from singed hair they were more or less uninjured.

Across an area of 230 square miles everything was levelled. Whole buildings disappeared, ancient cedar trees with trunks up to six feet in diameter were uprooted and thrown to the ground, and the local wildlife was virtually wiped out. As volcanic ash rained down on them, Nelson and Ruff sought shelter under a pile of debris, desperate to avoid being struck by rocks and car-sized lumps of ice hurtling out of the sky.

. . . desperate to avoid being struck by rocks and car-sized lumps of ice hurtling out of the sky

It took some time to collect their thoughts, and when they came out of hiding they could hear cries of help from two of their friends. Brian Thomas must have been struck by a tree branch flying through the air and thought he'd broken his hip. Dan Balch was so severely burned by the blast that the flesh appeared to be melting off his hands. He had lost his shoes and injured one leg but was able to walk with support, though Thomas wouldn't be going anywhere for the time being. The other two, Terry Crall and Karen Varner, were nowhere to be seen.

Before Balch slowly made his way down to the river to cool his burning skin, Nelson and Ruff helped him build a makeshift shelter for Thomas. They all assured their friend that they wouldn't abandon him, and with the eruption still continuing Nelson and Ruff set off to look for help.

Moving anywhere within the huge blast zone was exceptionally hard going. Everywhere for miles around was knee-deep in scorching ash, and Nelson and Ruff had to pull up their shirt collars to use as masks, but even then breathing was difficult.

For several hours the pair made slow progress, fallen trees making it impossible to travel in a straight line. It was hot and exhausting but they kept it up until dusk, when they were finally spotted by the pilot of a National Guard helicopter, who offered to fly them to safety.

The couple refused to climb aboard unless someone helped rescue their friends. With the volcano still spewing out ash and molten rock – more than five hundred million tonnes in total – the pilot took some persuading to fly up to the campsite. But when they got there and began searching it was impossible to tell where they had left Thomas. Everything that might have acted as a landmark was gone, the whole area swept away by the ferocity of the blast and then covered in debris. The great clouds of ash also made it impossible to see more than a few yards.

The couple refused to climb aboard unless someone helped rescue their friends

In such circumstances a thorough search was not possible, but after being airlifted to safety Nelson and Ruff were delighted to learn that their two friends had already been rescued by another detachment of the National Guard.

The last two were not so lucky. Tragically, Terry Crall and Karen Varner were listed among nearly sixty dead as a result of the catastrophe. They were killed almost instantly by a tree falling on their tent, although

in the chaos and confusion it took a while to locate their bodies. When rescuers finally came upon them the pair were found huddled together, Crall's arm wrapped protectively around his girlfriend.

Colby Coombs
The mountaineer who overcame an avalanche (Alaska, 1992)

In early summer Colby Coombs was holidaying in the Alaska Range, North America's highest mountains, which span more than four hundred miles and rise to over twenty thousand feet. An experienced mountaineer and wilderness guide, Coombs was climbing with his friends Tom Walter and Ritt Kellogg. Keen for a new challenge, the three wanted to explore a new route to the 17,400-feet summit of Mount Foraker. They made excellent progress until, on day four, a violent storm blew up out of nowhere.

Anywhere above thirteen thousand feet the weather can change the landscape in an instant. Within seconds the three men were effectively blinded by a condition known as a whiteout. With no time to seek shelter or consider their options, they were then hit by a sudden avalanche. When this happens there is little anyone can do except hope for the best. The trio were soon tumbling out of control before being thrown nearly eight hundred feet down a sheer rock face of the great mountain.

Knocked unconscious by the impact, it took more than six hours for Coombs to come round. When he did he was dangling at the end of a rope, scared but thankful he was alive. Fortunately, the rope was holding his weight, but his backpack was gone, along with his insulated mittens. His protective helmet was shattered, which gives an indication of the violence of the avalanche. He was also in serious pain from two fractured vertebrae in his neck and broken bones in one shoulder and ankle.

He was dangling at the end of a rope, scared but thankful he was alive

Slowly becoming more aware of his surroundings, he could see his companion Walter nearby. He too was hanging perilously from a length of rope, but there was no sign of Kellogg.

Even the smallest movement caused agony, but by using the weight of his body Coombs managed to swing closer to Walter. He could now see that Walter's head was encrusted in a mask of snow and ice and he began to fear the worst. After a few pendulum swings he was able to catch hold of his friend, but realised as he did so that he must have been killed by the fall.

The shock of losing a close companion in such a brutal way was awful, but Coombs felt grateful for the mask, which at least saved him the even greater distress of seeing his friend's face. This helped him view the incident more dispassionately, something which turned out to be crucial to his survival. Put simply, by treating the dead body as no more than that – just a body – he could concentrate fully on his own fight for survival. Mourning his friend, he decided, would have to wait until he was safe.

Mourning his friend, he decided, would have to wait until he was safe

Coombs knew he had to focus on getting down the mountain as quickly as possible. Above all, this meant not allowing himself to be distracted by panic or fear or the increasing pain of his injuries. He also knew it was important not to rush things. Cutting himself free of the rope, and still feeling dizzy from the fall, he thought it would be sensible to rest for a while. Having salvaged Walter's sleeping bag, he snatched a few hours' sleep on a narrow rock ledge.

Waking the following morning Coombs felt much calmer, and slowly lowered himself to the bottom of the escarpment using a rope technique mountaineers call rappelling or abseiling. It was here that he made a second terrible discovery when he found his other friend lying dead where he'd fallen. Once again he consciously struggled not to give in to grief. Instead, he set about salvaging and checking equipment – any ropes and supplies that might be useful. Before embarking on his solo descent down the forbidding Mount Foraker, Coombs cooked some food and melted snow for drinking water.

He would not give up until he had tried everything he possibly could to get home alive

He knew success would depend not only on his climbing knowledge and expertise but on a determination to focus solely on his personal survival. Coombs promised himself that he would not give up until he had tried everything he possibly could to get home alive.

He was sure his fear could be controlled by consciously avoiding all thoughts about dying. He also hoped to lessen his pain by thinking about the task ahead rather than his injuries.

Even so, his previous experience in the Alaska Range meant he was well aware of the dangers facing someone in his situation. At high altitude a peak as formidable as Foraker is always extremely dangerous. Such environments force even the fittest, best-equipped climbers to be vigilant. Coombs therefore had to be constantly alert to the dangers of stress, dehydration, exhaustion and exposure to the elements.

He believed his best chance of survival was to reach an area known as the Southeast Ridge. He would have to walk to get there, but he knew he couldn't put any weight on his shattered ankle. The frustration at how long it took to travel even short distances must have been immense, but trusting his sturdy boots to keep the splintered bones in place, Coombs hobbled on.

Several times he was forced to make lengthy and painful detours. On one occasion a fresh fall of snow meant inching his way back up the mountain in search of a new route around the deep snowfield; had he pressed on he might have triggered another deadly avalanche. Countless times his rope snagged or became frayed on rocky outcrops, and attempts to prevent himself slipping out of control caused even more pain as his broken bones were wrenched out of place.

Despite all this Coombs found the strength to continue

Despite all this Coombs found the strength to continue. Eventually, after several days, he found himself on the Kahiltna Glacier, a perilous ice channel more than forty miles long and riddled with hidden crevasses. But with no other choice open to him, he again set off on his long, slow walk.

If he could reach Denali base camp he knew he would find human company at last. Denali also had a temporary airstrip, set up on the ice for specially adapted aircraft to land and take off during the climbing season. It was in one of these planes that Coombs finally flew to safety, airlifted to a nearby hospital where he began his second long journey – the road to recovery. He spent the next three months in a wheelchair while doctors worked to repair his broken bones. Eventually he returned to the mountains and established a school to teach and promote climbing safety.

Eric LeMarque
The snowboarder who took a deadly wrong turn (California, U.S.A. 2004)

Eric LeMarque was a super-fit sports star who competed in the 1994 Winter Olympics. He had taken up snowboarding after retiring from professional ice hockey. It quickly became his passion, a thrilling hobby that gave him great pleasure and such an adrenalin rush that he had time for little else.

In 2004 LeMarque was snowboarding on Mammoth Mountain, an ancient and well-named volcano in California's Sierra Nevada range. Mammoth is nearly nine thousand feet high, and although it hasn't erupted for more than seven hundred years it can be a seriously dangerous place.

A few years ago a ranger was almost suffocated by gas leaking from the rocks, a gas so poisonous that it has killed thousands of trees. More recently, three members of an official ski-patrol team died after being overcome by natural carbon dioxide emissions escaping from the ground.

Such high peaks offer plenty of other perils too, and with nearly thirty-three feet of snow falling each year (easily enough to bury a house) Mammoth is no exception. LeMarque knew this but such was his addiction to his sport that when a storm warning forced the ski patrol to order everyone down from the slopes he decided he would take one more exhilarating ride before calling it a day.

It was this foolish decision that almost cost him his life.

It was this foolish decision that almost cost him his life.

A keen snowboarder like LeMarque would have known that ski-patrol orders need to be taken seriously, but this time he was thinking only that he wanted the last run of the day to be a good one. He realised that if he took such a risk there was a strong chance he would encounter thick fog on the way down. Still, he decided to hike further up the mountain before starting his run.

As he made his final high-speed descent this is exactly what happened:

running into a great bank of thick fog he found himself in terrain he could barely see let alone navigate.

This led him to make his second big mistake of the day when, completely disoriented, he turned the wrong way in the fog. He didn't know it but he was now heading deeper into the wilderness rather than towards a route off the mountain where he would have been safe.

It didn't take long for LeMarque to realise he was lost, but unable to see more than a few feet he couldn't retrace his steps. It was also beginning to get dark, which meant he would soon be in desperate trouble. He was alone on the mountain, in poor visibility, with the temperature plunging and no survival equipment.

In fact, he had no equipment at all, except his snowboard and an MP3 player and radio, which he liked to listen to while rocketing across the snow. He realised how serious his situation was, but for now there was nothing to be done. He would have to spend the night on the mountain, with no tent, no sleeping bag and no food. He had nowhere to shelter and nothing but the clothes he was wearing.

He had nowhere to shelter and nothing but the clothes he was wearing

If he slept at all it was for only a few minutes – months later all he could recall was that he couldn't stop shivering. The following morning his plan was to walk down the mountain; despite the storm and poor visibility, he felt sure he would find his tracks and follow his original route back to one of the ski lodges.

Unfortunately, he was wrong. His tracks had been obliterated by the storm, but in the silence he could at least hear running water, which was a huge relief. He had nothing to eat but he knew he had to find something to drink, and the river wasn't too far away. But as he knelt down to take a mouthful disaster struck.

The ledge LeMarque was kneeling on gave way and he was pitched into the river. In shock at suddenly finding himself in ice-cold water it took him several moments to work out what had happened, and several more to struggle back onto the bank. Scrambling out as quickly as he could, he was now wet through as well as freezing cold and very hungry.

Scrambling out as quickly as he could, he was now wet through as well as freezing cold and very hungry

His first thought was to strip off his clothes, after which he did a crazy, naked dance in the snow in an attempt to dry himself off and warm up. It worked up to a point, but afterwards he had no choice but to put his wet clothes back on.

With his body temperature decreasing he made very little progress before it began to get dark again. After finding a rock ledge to rest on, he knew he faced the ordeal of another night alone on the mountain.

Without any way of getting dry or warm, and the temperature dropping to well below zero, LeMarque woke the next morning to find that he'd lost much of the feeling in his hands and feet. Removing his boots and peeling back his socks, he was horrified to see that his feet were turning purple and black from severe frostbite.

It is possible to recover from bad frostbite, but only if the affected parts of the body are treated quickly. LeMarque knew there was no chance of

early treatment, and began to realise that even if he reached safety he might end up losing both his feet.

His other major problem was that he was still heading in the wrong direction. For someone with no food, badly injured feet and no specialist equipment he was making excellent headway, and on the third day he hiked as many as seven miles through the snow. But with such poor visibility he was heading away from safety, and it was only when the weather finally cleared that he realised it.

By now he was at least nine miles off course and knew he had no choice but to go back up the mountain and start all over again.

Incredibly, the injured and exhausted man found the mental strength to will himself on. It was increasingly tough and sometimes he could take only ten steps at a time – but he always made sure to take all ten steps before allowing himself to collapse into the snow for a rest.

Each night he used his snowboard to scoop out a shallow cave in the snow

Each night he used his snowboard to scoop out a shallow cave in the snow. The result was by no means warm or comfortable but it offered some protection against the worst of the mountain climate. In all, he survived seven nights. Towards the end of his ordeal he managed to sleep right through until morning because he was so tired it was impossible to stay awake.

On the morning of the eighth day he switched on his MP3 radio and heard that a local search and rescue team was combing the mountain looking for his body. The report gave him a huge shock: clearly no one who knew Mammoth believed that a snowboarder without food, shelter and survival equipment could still be alive after more than a week on the slopes.

This was all LeMarque needed to give him the renewed resolve to survive. No one had lasted more than two nights in similar conditions, but from that point on he prayed for the determination to get down the mountain no matter what

Even if he had to crawl on his hands and knees, he was not going to let his parents bury their son

it took. Even if he had to crawl on his hands and knees, he was not going to let his parents bury their son.

By now, as well as frostbite, he was showing symptoms of acute hypothermia, an often fatal condition which affects people when their body temperature falls to a dangerous level. Alongside finding it hard to breathe he was starting to hallucinate. Worse, the desire to lie down and sleep was so strong he could barely move.

In this condition it seems doubtful he would have made it home, no matter how strong his determination. But we can never be sure about this because while fighting the urge to take yet another rest beneath a snow-covered ridge he heard the faint sound of an engine.

Gradually the sound grew louder and louder, and then suddenly the air above him was ripped open by the deafening sound of a helicopter's spinning rotor. LeMarque was safe at last, but in terrible shape.

His body temperature was dangerously low and he was badly dehydrated. He had also lost an incredible forty pounds in a week. Once he was airlifted to safety his lower legs had to be amputated as a result of the frostbite.

Despite all this he made a remarkable recovery. After a long period of complex surgery Eric LeMarque – fitted with prosthetic legs – returned to Mammoth Mountain and his beloved snowboarding.

Craig Hosking
The pilot who crashed inside a volcano (Hawaii, 1992)

Craig Hosking works as a Hollywood camera pilot and has filmed many famous action scenes for blockbusters featuring characters such as James Bond, Batman and Indiana Jones. It's a dream job for someone like Hosking, who has been passionate about flying and photography for as long as he can remember – he was only sixteen years old when he qualified for a licence to fly helicopters.

In 1992 he was hired to fly cinematographer Mike Benson and camera technician Christopher Duddy. They needed to film scenes of boiling lava for a movie called *Sliver* and had chosen Kilauea, the most active of the five volcanoes on the island of Hawaii. The two men planned to spend one Saturday recording a large plume of smoke from a vent called Pu'u 'O'o, and a pool of glowing lava nearly a hundred feet inside the crater.

> The three men were instantly plunged into a dense cloud of smoke and steam from the volcano

Hosking flew the camera crew down into the six-hundred-foot deep crater several times, but on the third low-level pass the helicopter seemed to lose power. A warning light flashed on the control panel but the malfunction was so sudden that the three men were instantly plunged into a dense cloud of smoke and steam from the volcano. Emerging from the cloud moments later Hosking realised he had no choice but to land the helicopter immediately.

With just seconds to act before the loss of power became catastrophic, Hosking's professional experience told him that flying clear of the volcano was out of the question. He also knew that he couldn't land too close to the pool of boiling lava. If he did the steep gradient would cause the helicopter to roll over, which would almost certainly kill all three of them. The only option was to aim for a flat area close to the centre of the crater.

Hosking's plan was far from ideal but he thought it might work as long as he could avoid the bubbling lava and another large area strewn with rocks.

During the helicopter's rapid descent, the main rotor struck the crater wall

Unfortunately, during the helicopter's rapid descent, the main rotor struck the crater wall and broke free of the fuselage. Hosking managed to get the machine down in one piece, but the men were now stranded inside the volcano and at least 150 feet below its rim.

When they emerged, dazed and in shock, from the crumpled wreck of the helicopter, they saw what looked like a scene from one of the disaster movies they helped create. The air was thick with choking, poisonous fumes, and the sound from the molten rock bubbling up to the surface added to the fearsome display. At times it made ominous gurgling noises, at others it was like waves breaking on shingle. In the gloom of their rocky prison they witnessed a terrifying lightshow from the eerie glow of the boiling lava pool.

All three realised that the gases surrounding them were extremely dangerous. These included hydrogen sulphide (which is poisonous, highly corrosive, flammable and explosive) and a toxic irritant called sulphur dioxide. A little fresh air seemed to be coming down from the rim, but suffocation was a very real prospect unless they got out of the volcano soon. There was no sign of a rescue party yet, so Duddy and Benson decided to scale the walls of the volcano in the hope that they might find a way out. Hosking, meanwhile, chose to remain with his wrecked helicopter, believing he could repair its damaged radio and call for help.

Duddy and Benson quickly found that climbing up the inside of a crater was a nerve-wracking challenge – neither had any experience of this sort of thing, let alone any expertise. The brittle walls of the crater were crumbling, and any careless move could easily start a landslide that would carry them deeper into danger. Treading very slowly and carefully they made their way up the crater, but soon became separated, stranded on ridges at least sixty feet short of the rim.

Hosking was having better luck. Working in the choking air, after several setbacks he eventually fixed the helicopter's emergency radio and summoned help. When a courageous local pilot risked a second flight into the crater Hosking scrambled aboard.

Rescuing the other two men was much harder. Benson decided that the most sensible option was to sit tight and wait for a rescue team. The air was cleaner at this height, and he felt that continuing the climb would be too dangerous. Instead, he secured himself in a narrow crevice and waited for help to arrive.

Duddy chose the alternative. Convinced he would die if he stayed in the crater much longer, he opted to struggle on towards the rim. At one point during his slow ascent he had a terrible

Convinced he would die if he stayed in the crater much longer, he opted to struggle on towards the rim

shock: a man-sized object suddenly appeared through the gaseous cloud before crashing to the bottom of the crater. Horrified, Duddy thought it was one of his companions falling to a violent death. In fact, it was proof that a rescue attempt was at last underway. The large object was a survival pack, thrown over the rim in the hope that it might land close to the men trapped below.

The incident badly unsettled Duddy, but eventually he reached the rim at around two-thirty the following afternoon. Coughing and wheezing from the effect of the gas, he was at least safe, like Hosking. But more than twenty-four hours into the ordeal Benson was still trapped in his crevice and was beginning to suffer.

Having lost contact with the other two, his biggest fear was that he might now be the only one still alive. This made him even more anxious about his chance of being rescued, and the sound of volcanic activity below only unnerved him even more. He tried to take his mind off these fears by using little tricks, such as reciting the alphabet backwards. He had no food

Benson started hallucinating, imagining he could see the figure of Pele, Hawaii's spiteful goddess of volcanoes

and hadn't eaten for many hours, but by cupping his hands and reaching out from the crevice he was able to catch some rainwater to drink.

At one point Benson started hallucinating, imagining he could see the figure of Pele, Hawaii's spiteful goddess of volcanoes. He thought she was reaching out to him across the crater, but fortunately he still had some fight left in him. More than once he got to his feet and screamed at her to leave him alone.

By Monday morning Benson was still trapped, but then the haze and smoke cleared momentarily. The improved visibility enabled the pilot of another helicopter to spot the missing man, if only for a second or two. With the smoke thickening once more Benson's shadowy form vanished as quickly as it had appeared, but at least the rescue team knew his approximate position.

Flying down into the crater for a third time was considered too dangerous in the circumstances. Instead, a large net at the end of a 150-foot cable was slowly lowered towards the ridge. Manoeuvring it into position required expert flying and it took a while to get it right. Finally Benson managed to reach out to the net and clamber into it. By mid-morning, nearly two full days after the initial helicopter flight had come to grief, he was airborne once again and on his way to the nearest hospital.

Benson managed to reach out to the net and clamber into it

Nearly a week later Benson was still coughing painfully, but, remarkably, he and the other two men suffered only a few minor cuts and bruises. Following an ordinary crash landing this would have been an extremely lucky outcome, but after coming down inside an active volcano it seems nothing short of amazing.

Anna Bågenholm
The woman who froze to death – yet lived (Norway, 1999)

While taking a break from her long medical training to become a surgeon, Anna Bågenholm fell into danger when skiing on one of her favourite mountains in the beautiful countryside near Narvik in northern Norway.

It was a warm spring evening in the Kjølen Mountains and the twenty-nine-year-old was enjoying herself with two friends, who were also doctors. Suddenly, as she tried to steer a path around a waterfall, she fell head first into a fast-moving stream. The water wasn't deep but she was trapped between thick ice and rocks, struggling to breathe,

Her friends tried to pull her free but were unable to move her. One of them battled to keep a grip on Bågenholm's wet skis, desperate to prevent her being pulled further under, and the second called for help on her mobile, aware that her stricken friend was being pummelled by an unstoppable torrent of ice-cold water tumbling down the mountainside.

Fortunately, in what would otherwise have been a deathtrap, Bågenholm found a pocket of air beneath the ice. This allowed her to keep breathing, although it couldn't protect her from the cold. As the minutes wore on and no help came, she gradually lost consciousness. After forty minutes her friends were left clinging to what appeared to be a lifeless body.

After forty minutes her friends were left clinging to what appeared to be a lifeless body

It took a while longer for the first of two rescue teams to reach the narrow gully. A rope was attached to Bågenholm's legs to hold her fast, then the rescuers began using a snow shovel and a small saw to break through the eight-inch-thick ice. It was slow work but eventually, when a second team arrived with a larger, more pointed shovel, they were able to pull her free.

By now Bågenholm had been trapped underwater for around eighty minutes. She wasn't breathing and no one could feel a pulse, which meant her heart had stopped beating and her blood was no longer flowing. Shining a bright light into her eyes produced no response, a worrying sign suggesting that she had died from a combination of the freezing temperature and a lack of oxygen.

The nearest hospital was an hour away by air, but the huddled group on the mountainside refused to give up. Waiting for a helicopter to arrive, they made repeated attempts to revive their patient, but she remained white-faced and completely motionless. Standard practice for such an incident includes the kiss of life, chest compression and other first-aid techniques known collectively as cardiopulmonary resuscitation, or CPR – but none seemed to be having any effect.

The huddled group on the mountainside refused to give up

Still showing no signs of life, Bågenholm was lifted into the helicopter and flown to Tromsø University Hospital, more than two hours after her fall. The symptoms she displayed were immediately familiar to hospital staff. It looked like hypothermia: when the body temperature drops below 30°C most people lose consciousness, and at 25°C a heart attack is likely. Without medical treatment death can follow very quickly.

Bågenholm's temperature had dropped to an astonishing 13.7°C. She was an exceptionally severe case, although the condition is far from rare in this part of Scandinavia. The city of Tromsø is well within the Arctic Circle, and snowfalls of nearly eight feet have been recorded there. Local hospitals frequently treat people with hypothermia, but when the emergency staff were still unable to detect a pulse they knew that this was no ordinary situation.

The good news was that the air pocket had prevented Bågenholm from drowning, but now the hospital had to launch a long and complex procedure to see if there was any chance of bringing the patient fully back to life. The assembled doctors and nurses knew that in all the previous

cases of hypothermia they had treated no one had ever recovered from such a dramatic drop in temperature.

In a specially designed operating theatre Bågenholm was hooked up to a sophisticated bypass (heart-lung) machine and a video probe was inserted into her chest to monitor her heart. While resuscitation attempts continued, the blood was carefully drained from the veins, fed through the machine and then gently pumped back into her arteries. The hope was that by gently warming the blood, they would gradually return the patient to a normal temperature and regained consciousness.

No one had ever recovered from such a dramatic drop in temperature

By now there had been no signs of life for more than four hours, but then a faint heartbeat was detected and shortly afterwards confirmed. Over a period of nine hours Bågenholm's pulse slowly strengthened as nearly a hundred medical personnel worked to complete the process of bringing her brain and body back to full consciousness.

It was clear, however, even when her heartbeat normalised and she opened her eyes several days later, that she was far from well. There were no obvious signs of injury, no broken arms or legs, but she was unable to move any of her limbs. Her kidneys and digestive system were also not functioning properly, and for at least two months she remained in the hospital's intensive care unit. Hooked up to a variety of medical equipment, she needed round-the-clock specialist treatment.

Crucially, she had suffered no brain damage, an amazing outcome for someone who had exhibited no signs of life. It is not possible to explain this medical miracle with any certainty, mostly because no one else has ever recovered from a body temperature as low as 13.7°C. For this reason Bågenholm's case continues to be closely studied by doctors around the world. Many valuable lessons have been learned about how to save the lives of people suffering strokes, liver failure and epilepsy, as well as severe hypothermia.

However, Bågenholm's medical team think they might know the reason for her extraordinarily good fortune. In one very important regard they believe the exceptionally cold temperature under the ice might have worked to their patient's advantage. For some time doctors have known that a cool brain needs less oxygen than a warm one, and Bågenholm might, in effect, have been able to hibernate during the hours following her fall into the icy stream.

Ordinarily such a thing would never happen, but perhaps the unusual nature of her accident allowed Bågenholm's body to cool down completely before her heart stopped functioning. If her brain was sufficiently cold its individual cells would require very little oxygen. In this way her brain was able to survive for several hours, and in circumstances which otherwise might have killed even the fittest person.

Her brain was able to survive for several hours

Bågenholm was certainly fit but her recovery and return to good health nevertheless took more than a year. Even then, it was never quite complete. Some of the damage to the nerves in her hands and feet turned out to be irreversible, and sadly this meant she had to abandon her dream of becoming a surgeon. Fortunately, she was able to retrain as a radiologist, a doctor who specialises in medical investigations and treatment using techniques such as X-rays and ultrasound scans.

Once qualified in radiology, Anna Bågenholm began working with the very doctors and nurses who saved her life, and alongside one of her friends from that fateful day, who is now a member of the Tromsø University Hospital helicopter emergency team. Happily both have returned to the slopes many times and continue to enjoy skiing in some of northern Europe's most breathtaking and unspoiled landscape.

JOHANN WESTHAUSER
The caver who got trapped for a dozen days (Germany, 2014)

When a team of German explorers first stumbled into their country's deepest cave system twenty years ago they were so amazed by its immense size that one of them gasped, *'Es ist eine Riesensache'*

('It is a giant thing'). The title was officially adopted and today the Riesending, nicknamed the Everest of the Deep, is something of a legend among spelunkers, or potholers.

Adventurers travel to this corner of south-eastern Germany to test their caving skills in a series of caverns which run more than twelve miles beneath the Bavarian Alps. Others, such as Johann Westhauser, who was among that original group of explorers, are professional scientists. Their objective is to accurately map this staggeringly complex labyrinth of tunnels and underground rivers, which cuts vertically and horizontally into the mountains.

These scientists have been working on this for more than a decade, but the task is so huge that the survey is nowhere near complete. Hundreds of tunnels have not yet been measured, and the search is still on for a link through a 'super cave' to the Kolowrat system across the border in Austria. Another vast maze thought to be as long as fifty miles, it includes an estimated four thousand individual caverns and passages.

Westhauser had been studying the caves for nearly twelve years when he was injured in a sudden rockfall. At the time **He was at least four miles from the entrance to the caves** he was at least four miles from the entrance to the caves. The heavy boulder had fallen a considerable distance, as much as fifty feet, and despite wearing a helmet the fifty-two-year-old sustained a serious head injury.

As well as a fractured skull and eye socket, Westhauser suffered a dangerous haemorrhage and was losing blood from the part of the brain that controls arm and leg movements.

Under normal circumstances any doctor examining him would have ordered an immediate airlift to hospital and emergency treatment in a specialist intensive care unit. But conditions in the Riesending were far from normal. To reach safety from where the scientist lay drifting in and out of consciousness would have taken an expert caver the best part of a day. Westhauser was certainly an expert, but in his present condition he was unable to stand let alone climb.

Realising it would be unsafe to move him, one of his colleagues began the long, slow ascent to get help. Getting to the surface took him ten hours, an astonishing achievement for someone climbing solo. Ascending alone in such an environment is far more strenuous than working as part of a team, and it invariably involves taking far greater risks.

Getting to the surface took him ten hours, an astonishing achievement for someone climbing solo

Once he reached the surface a specialist rescue team was quickly assembled. The first to arrive were members of the local mountain rescue service, but this situation was far outside their experience. This time the victim was not lying at the top of a mountain but marooned in a cave thousands of feet below ground. The recovery operation would require additional skills, and it was left to the expert cavers and climbers to begin making their way down into the cave system.

Reaching the stricken Westhauser took almost as long as it had taken to sound the alarm. The journey into the depths involved abseiling on ropes down vertical shafts hundreds of feet deep and crawling along tortuous horizontal sections. To make it even harder, some of the pinch points, or bottlenecks, in these tunnels are so tight that cavers have to breathe out in order to squeeze through them. And everything had to be done in semi-darkness, while knowing that the risk of another rockfall was ever present.

It was crucial to get a doctor to the scene, but the first one who tried to reach Westhauser was beaten back by the difficulty of the descent. Finally, after many more hours, another was able to get through. The patient, he reported, was in a bad way: conscious but with such a serious brain injury that moving him straightaway was out of the question. Instead, he needed to be stabilised to prevent him succumbing to hypothermia from the damp and ice-cold atmosphere underground, the risk being much higher because he was immobile.

The seriousness of Westhauser's injuries meant that he would not recover quickly enough or sufficiently to make his own way out. And owing to the convoluted cavern system, even with the right equipment it would be impossible to winch the injured man to the surface.

He would have to be brought out with the assistance of other cavers working their way slowly through the network of passages and tunnels. Fortunately, by this time specialists from Switzerland and Austria were arriving on the scene, along with many from the local area. They were joined by other volunteers from Italy and Croatia, the mercy mission eventually involving an incredible 728 men and women, as well as several helicopters. These were kept busy flying supplies and equipment up to the cave entrance nearly 6,000 feet above sea level. Initially everything had to be lowered to the ground by ropes and cables until it was possible to clear a makeshift landing area.

From the start, everyone co-ordinating this massive rescue effort realised it would take several days to complete, if indeed it was possible. It was by far the most complex operation of its sort ever undertaken. There were doubts it could be pulled off successfully, though with the patient in such a serious condition there was no alternative but to try.

A day and a half after the rockfall Westhauser was still suffering blackouts. Because of his fragile state his rescuers decided that with such a long ascent the evacuation would have to be broken down into a series of short stages. Completing each stage would be made even harder as the patient needed to be kept horizontal wherever possible. The doctors insisted this was necessary to prevent his injuries deteriorating.

After much discussion about the advantages and disadvantages of the various options it was decided that nearly a hundred climbers and cavers, working in teams of around fifteen, would carry the injured man. Travelling inch by inch through several miles of tunnels, each team would be accompanied by a doctor carrying a skull drill. This gruesome piece of equipment, which is exactly what it sounds like, might be needed to prevent a dangerous build-up of pressure if there was any more bleeding from Westhauser's brain.

Even with all the activity and the many hundreds of professionals and volunteers working above and below ground it took another five days before any attempt was made to begin the evacuation. In preparation for his gruelling ascent, Westhauser was checked and rechecked, and then securely strapped into a

It took another five days before any attempt was made to begin the evacuation

special stretcher used to transport injured skiers and mountaineers. He was also wrapped in a sleeping bag, together with several layers of styrofoam padding to protect him against the cold. This far down the temperature hovers around 3°C, though the freezing winds whistling through the caves make it feel far colder.

The styrofoam would also provide some protection from any knocks and bumps sustained during the course of a fiendishly complicated journey. While every attempt would be made to keep the patient steady and stable, it was inevitable in the tight confines of the narrowest tunnels that his body would need to be tilted, risking contact with the jagged, unyielding limestone of the rock walls.

His words were often slurred, but the good news was that he appeared not to have lost his memory

The swelling in his brain made it hard for Westhauser to speak. His words were often slurred, but the good news was that he appeared not to have lost his memory. Had he done so it would have indicated much greater damage to his brain and reduced the chances of him making a full recovery if his escape from the cave was successful. Happily, when asked a series of questions, Westhauser had no difficulty recalling that the World Cup was taking place in Brazil at the time of his accident. He even told the doctor that he didn't wish to know the score in a recent match as he wasn't at all interested in football!

Manoeuvring what was basically a dead weight through several miles of caves was exceptionally slow work, even with the ingenious system of ropes, levers, winches and pulleys set up along the escape route. Westhauser's injuries ruled out using the electric motor to lift him. Instead, his rescuers had to rely on their own muscle power, at times using their own bodies as counterweights to make the lifting a little easier.

At the start of the operation the most optimistic estimate was that it would take a week to bring Westhauser to the surface. In fact, his heroic rescuers managed to do it in just five days, the teams moving through the passages at an average speed of around 165 feet an hour, or about a quarter of the speed of a tortoise.

After twelve days so far underground and seriously injured, this was nothing short of miraculous

Once at the surface, Westhauser was carefully loaded onto a police helicopter and flown to a nearby hospital. Following a thorough examination, medical staff were confident that his brain would heal without surgery, and that after a fortnight or so in hospital their patient would be fit enough to return home. After twelve days so far underground and seriously injured, this was nothing short of miraculous.

JOHN CAPES
The survivor no one believed
(Greece, 1941)

During the Second World War submarine crews faced many dangers while on patrol in the Mediterranean. The subs were often unreliable and the clear water made it hard for them to hide from low-flying aircraft or vessels passing overhead. Hunted day and night by enemy ships and frequently bombed from the air, the men who ventured into the seas of southern Europe found themselves under almost constant threat of attack.

In December 1941 HMS *Perseus*, a Royal Navy sub, was travelling from Malta to Alexandria in Egypt. The neatly bearded John Capes was a member of the crew and held the rank of leading stoker. This meant he was one of the mechanics responsible for keeping the engines working, a job involving routine maintenance as well as sustaining a reliable fuel supply for the submarine's diesel generators.

Perseus had surfaced a few miles from the Greek island of Kefalonia; her captain was taking advantage of the darkness to recharge the batteries for the following day's patrol. As the sub came under attack, thirty-one-year-old Capes was lying on a makeshift bunk converted from an empty torpedo tube. When he felt the force of a huge explosion it was obvious to him that they'd struck an enemy mine. As an experienced sailor, he wasn't surprised when the sub immediately began to sink.

When he felt the force of a huge explosion it was obvious to him that they'd struck an enemy mine

Perseus came to rest on the seabed moments later. Capes was unhurt, and so far there was no sign of water pouring into his compartment. However, in those days it was virtually impossible to get out alive from a stricken submarine, which Capes would have known. Besides the risk of drowning, the pressure in deep water was enough to crush anyone who left the protective hull of the vessel. Records show that, in nearly six years of war, there were only four successful escapes from British submarines lying damaged on the ocean floor.

The lights went out a few seconds after the sub hit the bottom.

Plunged into darkness, Capes was then thrown violently out of his bunk and across the cabin. Moments later the submarine began filling with freezing, filthy water. Pulling himself up off the floor, he shone a torch around. In the thin beam the shocked sailor could make out the corpses of several shipmates. He was also aware of creaks and leakages in the submarine's structure, alarming evidence of damage from the huge pressure of the water now surrounding it.

Capes tried to move along the submarine, but the first hatch he tried to open was jammed shut. This could have been caused by the pressure of the water, damage from the blast or the impact of the sub hitting the bottom. Forcing it open would be impossible, so he quickly turned back the other way. When he came across three of his fellow stokers he detected faint signs of life. Pausing to grab four sets of the navy's standard-issue submarine escape apparatus, he courageously dragged the men one by one towards another escape hatch.

He courageously dragged the men one by one towards another escape hatch

Capes worked frantically to fit the apparatus onto his confused, semi-conscious shipmates, but the air was beginning to run out and he was now struggling to breathe. The escape apparatus – including buoyancy bag, oxygen bottle, mouthpiece and goggles – was designed to keep the user alive as they swam to the surface. Attaching this kit was tricky at the best of times, but with no help from the injured men it was desperately difficult. Holding the torch between his teeth, Capes did the best he could before pulling on his own apparatus and taking a vital gulp of life-saving oxygen.

According to Royal Navy regulations the escape apparatus was officially rated for use at one hundred feet below sea level, but the submarine's instruments now showed *Perseus* lying at almost three times this depth. No one had ever escaped from such a depth before, but Capes had no time to worry about this. He still needed to find a way out before he could begin to ponder whether or not he might reach the surface alive.

The strong steel hatches on submarines can be opened only when the pressure is equal on both sides. To reach this state the submarine needs to be flooded, meaning that Capes had to endure several nerve-shredding moments as the water around him rose up to his chin, his eyes and then over his head. It was only when the water reached right up to the hatch that he was able to twist the damaged levers and release it, giving it a massive shove to force it open.

He found time to take a quick glug of rum for courage, and then all he could do was pray that he could reach the surface in time

With the hatch pushed back as far as it would go, Capes had only a few seconds to manhandle his comrades through the aperture before following them out. Incredibly, he found time to take a quick glug of rum for courage, and then all he could do was pray that he could reach the surface in time. His concerns were that his air supply would run out or his chest and lungs might collapse from the immense pressure of the deep water.

Fortunately, once clear of the submarine, his body's natural buoyancy

propelled him to the surface at great speed. In just over a minute the cool night air hit his face: he had made it. The relief must have been intense, but so was the pain. Capes felt dizzy as the blood rushed to his head, and his lungs seemed to scream out for clean, fresh air. At the same time his body felt as though it had been ripped open by the force of rising through the water so rapidly.

He was frightened too, realising that he was alone in the middle of the cold, dark sea. There was no light to see anything by, and he couldn't hear anything either, except the lapping of the water and the sound of his breathing. There was no sign of the other three stokers, which meant that Capes was the sole survivor of the fifty-nine officers and men on board HMS *Perseus*.

Capes was the sole survivor of the fifty-nine officers and men on board HMS *Perseus*

As his heartbeat gradually returned to normal and his eyesight adjusted to the dark he could see pinpricks of light on the distant shore. He still had the torch and tried using it to flash an SOS message in the direction of Kefalonia. The island was occupied by enemy troops. They were mostly Italian but included around two thousand Germans. Capes would have known that he might be taken prisoner, but unless someone came to find him he would have to swim the considerable distance to the shore.

For the next five or six hours he slowly paddled his way towards the beach. It was getting light now and from a few hundred feet offshore he thought he saw a sentry surveying the horizon. He was lucky enough to reach the beach without being spotted, then quickly found a small cave to hide in and recover his strength.

His second lucky break came later that morning when two fishermen from a nearby village entered the cave, where they stored their nets. Surprised to find someone hiding there, they returned an hour or so later with food and dry clothes. Unable to speak English, and with Capes speaking no Greek, they gestured that they would wait until dark before attempting to smuggle him somewhere safer.

Exhausted by his narrow escape, he was taken inland and spent two weeks recuperating in a small village. Not everyone there trusted him, and many thought he might be a spy, but others kept him fed and watered and hid him whenever enemy soldiers came to search the area. When he felt fit enough to travel they lent him a donkey, but only on condition that he wouldn't kill it for food. He was also advised to dye his hair and beard black before leaving, to make himself appear a bit more like the locals.

If Capes were caught he would almost certainly be shot, so he travelled mostly by night. He spent more than a year moving from one small village to the next, trying to stay one jump ahead of the Italian search parties that regularly patrolled the countryside.

Everywhere he went he was hidden by courageous Greeks, ordinary families prepared to defy the occupying forces by harbouring an English sailor. Most of them were very generous and shared their food, although the war meant there was not much to spare and he gradually lost a lot of weight.

Everywhere he went he was hidden by courageous Greeks

It was May 1943 before the stick-thin Capes was finally able to get off the island. One night, under cover of darkness, he was smuggled out in a fishing boat. With the assistance of the Royal Navy, and travelling a roundabout route via Turkey, he finally made it to Alexandria, the submarine's intended destination.

Unfortunately, after all this, no one believed he had even been on the *Perseus*! Capes had a reputation as a lively and enthusiastic storyteller, and the details tended to change slightly each time he told his tale. This, and the fact that no one had ever escaped from such a depth before, meant

His version seemed so far-fetched that no one was prepared to take his word for it

many of his fellow sailors thought he had made up the whole thing. They knew about the tragic loss of HMS *Perseus*, but none of them could explain how he could have got to enemy-occupied Kefalonia from Malta. His version seemed so far-fetched that no one was prepared to take his word for it.

Before the end of the war Capes was awarded the British Empire Medal, but even when he died forty years later not everyone thought he deserved it. For the next decade his story was more or less forgotten, but then a group of divers made a remarkable discovery when they located the wreck of the *Perseus*. On board they found the depth gauge, the first hatch jammed closed, the remains of his makeshift bunk, and even the bottle of rum from which Capes had taken that final fortifying swig.

Scraping the glass clear of more than half a century of seaweed and grime, one of the divers also saw that the gauge was still reading 270 feet, exactly as the old sailor had always said it would. Confirmation came too late for John Capes, but today, at last, the submariner's supposedly impossible escape is rightly regarded as one of the most extraordinary survival stories of the entire war.

Leonid Rogozov
The doctor who operated on himself (Antarctica, 1961)

For two years Leonid Rogozov was a member of a Russian scientific team based at the Novolazarevskaya polar research station in Antarctica. The team was small, only thirteen people, and Dr Rogozov had taken a break from his formal surgical training to join them as the station medic.

The research station is located in a region of Antarctica called Queen Maud Land, after Queen Victoria's granddaughter, who married the King of Norway. The remoteness and ferociously cold climate mean it's cut off from the rest of the world for months at a time, and for much of the year it can't be reached by either air or sea. Scientists working at the station have to be completely self-sufficient. For example, should one of them become ill it would be impossible to reach a hospital. It was Rogozov's responsibility to diagnose what was wrong and provide appropriate treatment.

Unfortunately, in April 1961 it was Rogozov himself who fell ill. At first the twenty-six-year-old felt weak and a little sick, but within a few hours his temperature was rising alarmingly. By the following morning he had sharp pains in his side. These symptoms were familiar to him and he had little difficulty diagnosing their cause. He was suffering from appendicitis, a dangerous inflammation of the appendix, which is part of the digestive system.

By the following morning he had sharp pains in his side

The usual treatment involves surgical removal of the affected organ. The appendix is small, about four inches long, and the operation is a common one. Known as an appendectomy, it's also relatively straightforward when performed by a trained surgeon. In Antarctica, however, the nearest Russian-speaking surgeon was based at a second research station more than a thousand miles away. The quickest way to reach him would have been by air, but a blizzard had been raging across Queen Maud Land for several days, making it impossible for any aircraft to take off or land.

No doctor would recommend anyone operating on himself, but Rogozov knew that if left untreated his diseased appendix would quickly rupture and then burst. This would be as painful as it sounds, but also dangerous – so dangerous that he would die without immediate surgery. His temperature had already reached an alarming level, and soon Rogozov was vomiting repeatedly, indicating that his condition was becoming very much worse.

Thirty-six hours after he first noticed something was wrong, he knew that surgery was his only option – and that he would have to perform the procedure on himself, having never done it before or even seen it performed by other doctors.

He knew that surgery was his only option – and that he would have to perform the procedure on himself

With no expert staff on hand to help him, he had to ask some of his non-medical colleagues to assist. While two of them sterilised the surgical equipment and the room set aside for the operation, Rogozov showed a meteorologist how to work the retractors, which are used to hold the flesh back during surgery. The station driver was also brought in to help. His job would be to hold a mirror above the operating table so that Rogozov could see what he was cutting. Before beginning the procedure at 10 p.m., he explained to them that he must be revived as quickly as possible if he fainted from the pain.

A patient would normally be unconscious during an operation like this, but as surgeon and patient, Rogozov would have to do without a general anaesthetic. If he was to avoid making a fatal error he had to be even more alert than usual, and so allowed himself only a tiny dose of the very mildest painkiller. Anything stronger would interfere with his concentration.

The thought of cutting into himself must have been terrifying, but with no alternative the doctor–patient now lay back. Leaning slightly to the left he made a five-inch-deep incision in his right side. Without proper drugs the pain was excruciating, but Rogozov kept on. He then exposed the appendix so that he could see it in the mirror. The extraordinary pain was accompanied by waves of nausea and a growing sense of weakness, which made it hard for him to keep a tight grip on the scalpel.

For the next hour or so Rogozov needed to take frequent short breaks.

He knew that no matter how weak he felt, and no matter how bad the pain, he had to keep cutting

He knew that no matter how weak he felt, and no matter how bad the pain, he had to keep cutting. Looking up at the mirror he could see that his appendix had already begun to rupture and that there was an ugly hole at one end. It was large enough to stick his thumb through, meaning that the operation was not a moment overdue. As he finally cut out the appendix antibiotics were applied directly to the wound. After this he began to stitch up the wound before closing the deep incision in his side.

By midnight Rogozov had done all he could. Exhausted by the effort and in very great pain, now all he could do was hope that it was enough to save his life. After he was carried out of the improvised operating theatre he soon fell unconscious, leaving his assistants to clear up and wait for the morning to see how well or badly they had done.

For the next couple of days Rogozov's condition failed to improve. This is often the case after a long operation, even one performed under ideal conditions. On the fourth or fifth day, however, the patient at last began to recover. As his symptoms slowly diminished his temperature started to return to normal. Within the week he felt much fitter and was sufficiently confident enough to remove the stitches. When he did so he could see that the wound was clean and healing well.

Two weeks after falling ill Rogozov resumed his duties as station doctor, and within a month he was able to help with much of the heavy work that is routine on a polar research station. It took a while for news of his pioneering self-surgery to travel back to Russia, but when it was reported in the newspapers it made him something of a hero. Today, after more than half a century, his story continues to inspire young medical students, although the thought of having to endure such agony must horrify even the bravest of them.

The student who was sucked under by quicksand (Utah, U.S.A. 2011)

American student Rob Tesar was nearing the end of a twenty-five-day survival expedition, hiking and camping with three friends as they followed the course of Utah's Dirty Devil River. The group was travelling along a trail that led down to a section of bank on the eastern side of the river when they ran into trouble. The bank appeared to be mostly mud and sand rather than rock, but they were confident they could cross the river at this point. Tesar volunteered to go down and check it out.

He was about twenty feet clear of dry land when he noticed he was having difficulty moving his feet. Sensibly, he decided to turn back immediately, but before he could move any further his boots suddenly disappeared beneath the surface. Very quickly he found himself up to his knees in mud. One of his friends had also been sucked under, but fortunately only one foot was trapped in the ooze.

Tesar realised they had struck a patch of quicksand, a natural phenomenon that occurs when fine particles of sand are held together by friction in a slippery mess of mud and water. From a distance it looks perfectly ordinary, but when the mixture is disturbed, for example during an earthquake, the sand effectively liquefies, meaning it can no longer support any weight. Under the right circumstances the process needs only a small disturbance to set it off, and – as the two students were now finding out – it can be as little as the pressure of someone walking on it.

Tesar realised they had struck a patch of quicksand

Sometimes it's possible to spot quicksand by looking out for areas of ground without any vegetation, or large expanses of bright green moss. But hikers often don't realise what they're standing on until it's too late. The liquefaction takes just a second or two, which was what happened that afternoon on the bank of the Dirty Devil River.

The good news is that, unlike in films, the nature of quicksand means that anyone stepping onto it will sink only halfway, no matter how deep the sand or how heavy the person. The bad news is that once someone is stuck up to the waist it's impossible to climb out on their own. Bystanders can't help much either, since the strength needed to pull them out would be about the same as to lift a solid object weighing a tonne or more.

Unsurprisingly, the other two members of the group didn't know this and hoped they could pull them out. The main worry at this time was the weather. Eastern Utah in November is a chilly place, and with the temperature dropping to around 4°C at night anyone in wet clothes and unable to move is at serious risk of hypothermia.

After struggling to free themselves for about fifteen minutes, the two realised that all they were doing was wasting energy. Fortunately, their friends had a rope with them, as well as the equipment climbers use to lower themselves into narrow rock canyons. The two on the shore managed to rig up a pulley system, attaching one end of the rope to a secure rock on the bank in the hope they could use it to free their friends.

It took an hour, and with only one foot trapped in the quicksand it was eventually possible to pull the first of them free. Tesar wasn't so lucky. He was stuck fast and becoming exhausted. In an attempt to take the weight off his feet he managed partly to lie down on the sand. But this meant his clothes began to absorb water and his hands went numb from the cold in less than a minute.

By 3 p.m. it was colder still, with the sun beginning to sink behind the rocks of a nearby canyon. Aware of the dangers posed by the falling temperature they decided to activate a device designed for precisely this kind of emergency. A Personal Locator Beacon, or PLB, uses coded satellite signals to alert search and rescue parties to the location of someone in danger.

While waiting for help to arrive, Tesar's friends found pieces of driftwood and managed to build him a makeshift platform. By twisting round slightly he could rest his upper body and keep it out of the water. Hot food was also on its way, prepared using the group's portable stove. But Tesar was now desperately cold, and even after a warming meal of sausage, cheese and couscous his hands and lower body still felt numb.

By twisting round slightly he could rest his upper body and keep it out of the water

It was eight o'clock in the evening when they heard the distinctive sound of rotor blades echoing off the canyon walls. A helicopter touched down shortly afterwards, by which time Tesar was thigh-deep in the quicksand with the water almost up to his waist.

Initially the rescue crew decided to pull him free using the power of the helicopter. They threw straps and webbing across the sandbank and Tesar was instructed to make a harness. This would be attached to part of the helicopter and then, hovering just above his head, the pilot would gently ease him out of the quicksand.

It sounded good in theory: a powerful, modern helicopter versus several feet of wet sand, or man versus nature. Tesar felt confident that technical ingenuity would win the day, but he was wrong. He realised very quickly that far from lifting him free of danger, the helicopter was at risk of tearing him in half.

Signalling to the pilot, he brought the rescue attempt to an end. and little more than an hour after arriving at the scene the helicopter flew off to get further help. During this time several more hikers arrived, and Tesar tried to dig himself free using a shovel one of them had brought. This didn't work either. Unable to get sufficient leverage to dig properly, every time he managed to dig a little hole it quickly filled with the deadly mix of sand and water. Clearly he would have to rely on expert help rather than his own dwindling strength.

Far from lifting him free of danger, the helicopter was at risk of tearing him in half

When the helicopter reappeared it was carrying several inflatable rafts. Two were floated out to Tesar, each carrying four or five volunteers. While two of them supported his upper body as best they could, the remainder busied themselves trying to free his legs.

The work was hard and painfully slow. Half the rescuers were digging away with shovels, but just as important were the others who used their hands to prevent the sand and silt from the river flowing back into the spaces left behind. It was as if every effort to free Tesar from the oozing surface was matched by an equal effort on the part of the quicksand as it held on to its prey.

As midnight came and went Tesar was still stuck. Working fast but methodically, the diggers had been at it for well over half an hour. No one had taken a break yet they seemed to have made no progress. A third raft was positioned between the work party and the riverbank, so that Tesar could clamber onto it once he was out of danger. But nearing one o'clock in the morning it was still drifting empty.

It took a solid forty-five minutes of digging before Tesar thought he could feel any progress, and then suddenly he was sure of it. Although numb from the waist down, he told the diggers that his right boot had moved slightly. And when his leg seemed to shift he was even more confident that the rescue was working.

His leg hadn't moved more than an inch but it was enough to spur the diggers on. Desperate to loosen the quicksand's paralysing hold, and with everyone digging calmly but even faster than before, he pulled as hard as he could. At first nothing happened, but then one leg came up and seconds later the other did too. Tesar was finally free of the quicksand.

> Desperate to loosen the quicksand's paralysing hold, he pulled as hard as he could

Incredibly, it had taken nearly thirteen hours to wrestle him free, half the day and half the night since his boots had first slipped beneath the surface. It was another three days before the feeling returned to his legs, but with no permanent damage to his nerves – and no serious after-effects from the near-freezing temperature – Rob Tesar rejoined his group and went straight back out on the trail.

Greg Rasmussen
The conservationist who crashed in the Kalahari (Zimbabwe, 2003)

Greg Rasmussen is a conservation biologist and an expert on a particular species of wild dog. Known as 'painted dogs' – their distinctly patterned coats look like ink spots on blotting paper – they are one of Africa's top predators but in recent years have become increasingly endangered.

Around 150 of them live in the Hwange National Park, a vast wilderness where Rasmussen has spent more than twenty-five years studying their behaviour.

The dogs are closely related to wolves and jackals, and packs of them have lived in this part of southern Africa for at least three million years. They have a reputation for being better hunters than even leopards and lions, and once they spot their prey it rarely manages to escape. They work as a team and this helps them catch antelopes and other animals much bigger than them.

The dogs' territory is enormous and covers nearly six thousand square miles, much of it so hot and dry that entire lakes disappear each summer. This means scientists like Rasmussen have to travel huge distances to observe them, often in tiny aircraft called microlights. Many of the animals in Hwange have been fitted with radio collars, which makes them easier to locate using equipment carried in the microlights to pick up their signals.

One day in 2003 Rasmussen booked a pilot, as he needed to observe the dogs moving through the park. For some reason the pilot failed to show up, but this didn't trouble Rasmussen too much. He was more than capable of flying himself, and after completing the usual checks on the aircraft he took off shortly after dawn. Before long he picked up the first signal from a radio collar attached to a rhino. Noting the animal's position he pulled back on the controls and increased the power to climb to a higher altitude.

He was more than capable of flying himself, and after completing the usual checks on the aircraft he took off shortly after dawn

Suddenly, out of nowhere, he was hit by a sharp burst of air turbulence. One wing dipped downwards and the tail of the aircraft shot up. The next thing Rasmussen knew was that he was looking straight at the ground, which was getting closer and closer. In seconds the plane was in an uncontrollable spin. He could see rocks and trees looming ever larger, and then he heard a loud, sickening thump as it ploughed into the ground.

Rasmussen briefly lost consciousness, either from a blow to the head or the shock of the impact

Rasmussen briefly lost consciousness, either from a blow to the head or the shock of the impact. When he came round he was aware of blood and petrol running down his face. He couldn't feel his legs but he could wiggle his toes. He knew this meant he hadn't broken his spine and that he wasn't paralysed.

Modern aircraft are always fitted with radios and he was able to send an SOS. However, the impact had knocked the radio out of tune, and unable to retune it properly he had no idea whether anyone would hear his message. Instead of a friendly response telling him help was on the way, all he could hear was the ticking of the engine as it cooled down. That and the ominous sound of highly flammable fuel leaking out of the damaged plane.

Unable to move either of his legs, which Rasmussen correctly guessed were both broken, he knew he had to get out as quickly as possible – if the fuel caught fire he would be burned to death. Fortunately, his arms were uninjured and he was able to pull himself out of the cockpit and heave his body across the scorched ground to a safer position.

Lying around seventy miles from the nearest road, Rasmussen didn't need to be a wildlife expert to know that even if he moved away from the wreckage he was still far from safe. Until now he had never liked to refer to his beloved painted dogs as 'wild', for fear of reinforcing their reputation as nasty and brutal creatures. But as he lay in the broken shade of a thornbush he knew this reputation was well deserved. After all, these animals can survive without waterholes because drinking the blood of their prey provides them with all the nourishment they need. Rasmussen also knew that he faced other dangers besides the painted dogs. Hwange was also home to lions, leopards, cheetahs and hyenas, any one of which would attack a solitary, injured individual. Already several vultures were circling overhead.

The threat from the vultures would become even more serious after dark, but for now the biggest danger to his survival was dehydration. The park forms part of the Kalahari Basin, a region centred in an immense desert that takes its name from the local word *kgala*, meaning 'great thirst'. Here temperatures soar above 40°C and rainfall can be as little as two inches a year.

For now the biggest danger to his survival was dehydration

By now Rasmussen was hot and incredibly thirsty. Moving was out of the question, but even if he'd been able to search for something to drink the nearest waterhole might be miles away. It was awful to think that earlier that morning he'd pulled into a filling station, but because it was out of fuel he hadn't stopped to buy any water. Figuring he could get some on the way home, it hadn't occurred to him that he might be trapped out in the desert.

He was also in immense pain, especially from his legs and feet, which were bleeding profusely. He was desperate to get his boots off as quickly as possible to relieve the pressure and reduce the risk of infection, but he couldn't bend his legs to reach them. Undoing his laces took him more than an hour, loosening each one with a thin stick and slowly pulling it through the holes. Using a larger stick he was then able to push off one boot and then the other, but this took at least another hour.

Undoing his laces took him more than an hour, loosening each one with a thin stick

It was now midday and in the burning heat of the desert his lips were cracking badly and the dryness in his mouth was almost unbearable. With the sun at its highest the thornbush offered almost no protection at all. Rasmussen realised that his best hope of survival (assuming someone had heard his SOS) would be to wait out of the glare beneath the remains of the plane and hope that the fuel had all evaporated. As he hauled himself back across the ground he could hear his bones cracking. It was so agonising he began to suspect that he'd fractured his pelvis as well as his legs.

Moving very slowly he eventually made it, and at last the sun was beginning to set. This meant the temperature would fall to a more comfortable level, which would give him some relief from the terrible heat. Unfortunately, it also meant no one would be able to find him until dawn the next day, and that every large carnivore for miles around would now be out looking for something to eat.

Not too far away he could hear elephants. Like rhinos, they eat only vegetation but can be very dangerous if they decide to stampede. He knew his painted dogs hunted best by moonlight, and there were also the prowling hyenas to worry about. Above the sounds of the night he suddenly recognised the distinctive call of a lioness communicating with a lion.

Desperate to keep these big predators away, he felt his best chance was to make a lot of noise. Animals all seem to hate loud noise, so after beating hard on the plane's windscreen he started to drum on an aluminium strut to make as much racket as possible. When he stopped, the lioness came within six feet of him, but by keeping up the noise he managed to scare her off and somehow survive the night.

When he stopped, the lioness came within six feet of him, but by keeping up the noise he managed to scare her off

The next day looked like it was going to pass much like the first, only worse. Overnight Rasmussen had gone from being seriously thirsty to dangerously dehydrated. The pain from his lower body was increasing in severity too, and he was getting more and more worried that no one was coming to rescue him.

Perhaps the SOS message hadn't got through, or maybe it had but nobody could find the crash site or knew where to begin looking. Whatever the reason, he understood enough about this sort of place to know that he couldn't survive without water.

Fearing the end was near, Rasmussen spent some time thinking about his years working in the Hwange National Park. He felt them to have been among the best of his life. The experience of learning so much about the lives of painted dogs, and working to save them from extinction, had been enjoyable and a real privilege, even though the terrified locals referred to them as 'devil dogs'. His was a life that very few people got to experience, and it was something for which he was immensely grateful.

Lost in his thoughts, the weakening Rasmussen only slowly became aware of the drone of an aircraft. As it approached he tried to signal by waving a piece of wing spar, but the plane soon turned around. Closing his eyes, his spirits sank to a new low. He didn't know it but the pilot had already spotted something down below that looked like wreckage. He sent a radio message confirming this to the helicopter crew who were also scouring the area, and to a team on the ground approaching in an off-roader.

Pausing only to quench his insatiable thirst, Rasmussen was soon on his way out of danger

A few minutes later he was greeted by the first human voices he'd heard since his ordeal began. It didn't take long for the helicopter pilot to find a suitable spot to land. Pausing only to quench his insatiable thirst, Rasmussen was soon on his way out of danger. Nursing him back to health would take many months, however, and involved several dozen operations to rebuild his shattered bones. As a result of this his legs are now a couple of inches shorter, but he is back at Hwange and able to continue working with the painted dogs that mean so much to him.

BRANT WEBB AND TODD RUSSELL
The miners who spent two weeks underground (Tasmania, 2006)

For as long as man has been digging minerals out of the ground, mining has been one of the most dangerous of occupations. Sometimes miners are poisoned by gas leaks, or killed in explosions or when a tunnel collapses.

In 2006 on the Australian island of Tasmania it was a small earthquake that caused the calamity.

The quake occurred just after 9 p.m. It wasn't strong enough to do much damage at ground level, but below the surface the shock triggered a huge rockfall that threatened the lives of seventeen men. They worked in the Beaconsfield gold mine in the north of the island, and although fourteen of them managed to scramble to safety, three were trapped more than three thousand feet under ground.

Below the surface the shock triggered a huge rockfall that threatened the lives of seventeen men

One of the three was killed instantly by falling rocks, though it took another twelve hours or so for anyone on the surface to find this out. The other two, Brant Webb and Todd Russell, had been working with a heavy machine called a teleloader, which was used to erect barricades deep inside the mine. When the quake struck the two men were standing in its metal cage.

This almost certainly gave them some protection from the rockfall, but not much. Webb was knocked unconscious by a piece of falling rubble and Russell was buried in debris up to his waist. It took a few minutes for Webb to regain consciousness. Then, shocked and dazed, the two men struggled to free themselves from the broken remains of the teleloader. Some of the fallen debris was moved quite easily but much larger rocks refused to budge. Using a sharp pocketknife they managed to free themselves by cutting off any clothing caught between the boulders.

Above ground it took just minutes to establish that three men were missing. At this stage no one knew if they were alive or dead, and if they were alive whether anyone was injured. A rescue operation was quickly underway, and within a few hours a powerful, remote-controlled earth mover was working at the scene to clear fallen rocks from the tunnel where the men had been working. This was slow but effective, and news came the following morning that, via a camera mounted on the machine, the operator had spotted a body.

At this stage no one knew if they were alive or dead

It was soon identified as Larry Knight. He had been driving the teleloader when the earthquake occurred and was assumed to have died immediately after being hit by falling rocks. No one knew yet what had happened to the other two miners. To the gathering crowd on the surface, however, this tragic discovery must have shed doubt on whether either of them would be found alive.

The remote-control machinery continued working for a few hours more until it was decided the danger was too great to carry on. With so much loose rock to clear, the rescuers drew up plans to create a new access tunnel instead of trying to unblock the existing one. They thought this would be safer for the trapped men as well as members of the rescue team, even though it would have to be done using explosives.

Inside the mine Russell and Webb had water to drink, if only that which seeped down through the rocks. They collected it in their helmets, but for food they had only a small muesli bar. Initially they agreed not to touch it for the first twenty-four hours, before extending this deadline to two days and then three. When they finally unwrapped it they ate only tiny pieces to make it last as long as possible. Then Russell mislaid much of his share when a lump fell out of his pocket and disappeared in the dark.

Over the course of three days six controlled explosions were needed to open up the new tunnel, each one very frightening for the two men they were intended to free. While working hard on their side to clear the rocks, Russell wrote the time and date of each explosion on his torn overalls. This was in case he and Webb were killed in one of the blasts. He wanted their families and the rescue party to know that they had both survived the earthquake and had been trying to escape. The two miners also wrote short notes to their families, again on their overalls.

After four days trapped underground they were exhausted and extremely hungry. To take their minds off this, and to keep their spirits up, they sang more or less continuously, but as there was only one song they both knew they had to sing the same one over and over. Then, on the fifth day, one of them thought he heard voices. Two of their colleagues had ignored the safety warnings and were now approaching one section of the rockfall. They were calling out to Webb and Russell, who responded by shouting back as loudly as they could. Neither side could see each other, and with so much debris in the way it wasn't possible to have a proper conversation. But now everyone involved knew this was a rescue mission rather than an attempt to recover more dead bodies.

Around this same time a member of the forty-man rescue team was making his own attempt to reach the pair after returning to the spot where the remote-control excavator had stopped working.

Incredibly, by pulling at the rubble with his hands, he managed to open up a tiny hole. Soon he could fit his arm through it and eventually got close

After four days trapped underground they were exhausted and extremely hungry

enough to shake Russell's hand. This was an exciting development, but once again it was decided not to attempt to reach the men this way. It would have required cutting away part of the teleloader's ten-foot-long cage to clear a path out. But Russell and Webb feared this would cause another possibly fatal collapse of the many tonnes of rock resting on the cage roof.

It was still not possible to get the men out of their rock dungeon, but that first small hole quickly proved to be a lifesaver. Because of the exceptional hardness of the rock, and the amount of debris following the quake, everyone could see that it would be several more days before the men could be brought to the surface. By enlarging the hole, very carefully to avoid dislodging any more rocks, it was possible to feed a long length of flexible plastic tubing into the mine. Though only three and a half inches in diameter, this could then be used as a chute to supply the men with food and fresh water. The tube was also used to give them a walkie-talkie so they could communicate with the team working to free them.

Once the men had been provided with liquid food, vitamins and water, a new machine called a raise-borer was brought in. This is used for drilling what miners call a pilot hole, again one too small for anyone to fit through, but which allows a much larger grinding tool to be positioned to cut a proper escape tunnel just over three feet wide.

Despite all this equipment, the work to free the men was very slow. Even though geologists have calculated the rock in this area to be more than five times harder than concrete, special mining machines can cut through it at a rate of about three feet per hour. However, the operators were warned to work much more slowly than this in order to reduce the risk of causing another cave-in close to the men. As a result even boring the narrow pilot hole took the rescuers another three days, a delay that must have been agonising for the two miners.

Even boring the narrow pilot hole took the rescuers another three days

At some point during the rescue an iPod full of music was fed through the tube, along with details of a simple keep-fit programme. It was hoped these might prevent the men from becoming downhearted, as well as helping them pass the time.

For several days the work continued steadily if slowly, but then on the thirteenth day rescuers hit another problem when their cutting machine struck a belt of even harder rock. Attempts were made to break through it using jackhammers, or pneumatic drills, but when this failed it was decided to bring in more explosives. Once again there was a huge risk of setting off another rockfall, but they avoided this by using as little explosive as possible to fracture the last layer of rock.

A day later the rescue team knew they were within about three feet of the men. Between them lay another band of hard quartz rock, but for the first time everyone felt that the two miners were nearing the end of their imprisonment. The good news finally came just before five o'clock in the morning. After fourteen days underground Webb and Russell could see the lights on the helmets of their rescuers, and just ninety minutes later they were on the surface and hugging their families.

Before any celebration, their first duty was to be a very sad one: attending the funeral of their colleague and friend Larry Knight.

Neither Webb nor Russell escaped entirely without injury, but fortunately the damage to their backs and knees was relatively minor and would soon heal. It's almost impossible to imagine the experience of being incarcerated for so long, but it is one that will stay with both men for ever.

CLAUDIO CORTI
The climber who was snatched from the wall of death (Switzerland, 1957)

At just over thirteen thousand feet, the Eiger Mountain in Switzerland's Bernese Alps is well under half the height of Mount Everest. However, the ascent to the summit via the north face is one of the most dangerous climbs anywhere in the world, and more than sixty skilled mountaineers have died trying to reach the top.

Getting there from the west side is relatively easy for an experienced climber, and every year many men and women succeed. But for decades the north face defeated everyone who attempted it, and at one point so many were dying that the local authorities made it illegal for anyone to even try.

Known to mountaineers as the wall of death, the north face is almost vertical, making it exceptionally difficult to scale. For days on end, mountaineers are presented with nothing but bare rock, on which the so-called White Spider is the only feature to break the towering cliff's deadly monotony. Situated towards the top, this is a large ice field with several deadly snow-filled cracks radiating from the centre like a spider's legs. The exhausted climber must find a safe route through it in order to reach the top. Rockfalls are another serious danger and occur so regularly that many climbers prefer the winter months, when they hope that thick ice might strengthen the crumbling mountain.

Known to mountaineers as the wall of death, the north face is almost vertical, making it exceptionally difficult to scale

When Claudio Corti decided to attempt his ascent in 1957 no more than a handful of men had ever reached the summit via the north face. Many more had frozen, or fallen to their deaths or been swept away by avalanches. Young, strong and fit, Corti was undeterred by the danger. Together with another Italian, Stefano Longhi, he spent six days battling his way up the cliff before teaming up with a couple of German climbers, Franz Mayer and Günther Nothdurft.

All four were skilled mountaineers, but despite their experience and careful preparation the joint adventure ran into trouble almost immediately. Even in rare good weather the Eiger's north face is perilous, but falling

Falling temperatures made it look as though it was about to claim yet more lives

temperatures made it look as though it was about to claim yet more lives.

Longhi was the first to run into trouble. As the team approached an area of the cliff called Death Bivouac he found it harder and harder to keep moving. He was suffering the effects of frostbite at exactly the place where, a few years earlier, two other climbers attempting the north face had become lost in fog and froze to death.

Shortly after this disaster a second group of climbers had also come to grief in the same area. Falling more than 122 feet, one of its members somehow escaped serious injury, but his colleagues were less fortunate. One died of a fractured skull after being hit by falling rocks, and two more were subsequently found dead at the end of their ropes, dangling over the void.

Now Corti's group found themselves in similar difficulties when the stricken Longhi suddenly slipped and fell from a rock ledge known as the Traverse of the Gods. He was still attached to his colleagues by a rope but, exhausted and frostbitten, no one had the strength to haul him back up to the ledge.

They were forced to cut him free and he died of exposure. How long this took is impossible to say, but it was another two years before his body could be recovered and brought down from the mountain.

The next to meet disaster was Corti, who was hit by one of several falling rocks. His head wound was serious and he was unable to continue climbing or to retreat further down the mountain to a safer place. Unsure what to do with him, the two German climbers felt they had no option but to leave him behind and press on. If they could reach the summit, they thought, it would be possible to climb down the mountain using one of the easier routes and then organise a rescue party.

To give the injured Corti the best possible chance of surviving they left him a small red tent and all their supplies, but after this neither was seen alive again. Incredibly, both managed to reach the summit, even Nothdurft with his frostbite. Then, during their supposedly safer descent down the Eiger's west flank, they were hit by an avalanche and killed. It took four years before their bodies were recovered.

Corti meanwhile had his own battle to fight as he struggled to survive in the bitter cold for a terrifying four days. Huddled in a tiny tent on a slender rock ledge 820 feet below the summit, he had no choice but to stay put and hope someone would rescue him. Besides being too weak to climb, he'd given all his climbing equipment to Mayer and Nothdurft to increase their chance of making it home.

Though he was now very much alone, high up in the intense cold of the icy and exposed cliff, Corti's plight had not gone unobserved. In clear weather it's possible to view almost the whole of the north face from the ground; in fact, hotel guests in the nearby town of Grindelwald often use telescopes to watch climbers risking their lives.

Though he was now very much alone, high up in the intense cold of the icy and exposed cliff, Corti's plight had not gone unobserved

Corti didn't know it but he and his little red tent had already been spotted from a railway station thousands of feet below in the Kleine Scheidegg pass. Within hours a large group of volunteers was being assembled, and reporters and photographers were flocking to the area to witness what was to become the most daring Alpine rescue ever attempted.

Clearly it was not sensible to approach Corti from below. Doing this would have exposed the rescue team to exactly the same dangers that had befallen the four men, and many others before them. Instead the rescuers decided to climb the Eiger using the western route. They would then try and retrieve the injured Corti from the rocky ledge on which he was perched.

This mission took skill, strength and immense courage, and it involved no fewer than fifty-four people. Among them was another German, Ludwig Gramminger, who is now recognised as one of the heroes of mountain rescue. Gramminger pioneered the development of a special steel cable, which he now used to lower a mountain guide called Alfred Hellepart down from the top of the rock wall.

This mission took skill, strength and immense courage, and it involved no fewer than fifty-four people

Even supported by the cable, Corti was nowhere near fit enough to climb to safety. Besides his injuries and exhaustion, after nine days on the Eiger without food he had lost around 45 pounds and was dangerously close to collapse. Unable even to speak clearly, he was hoisted onto Hellepart's back before the guide slowly made his way back up the face as the cable was winched to the summit.

Corti was safe but delirious, and for many hours his conversation was incoherent and confused. For a while he even insisted he was the first Italian ever to conquer the north face, until it was politely pointed out that he'd made it to the top only after being carried there by a German. His recovery took several weeks, but eventually he was able to return to the mountains. When he did, he proved himself once more to be a strong and resourceful climber but, still haunted by the White Spider, he never returned to the north face of the Eiger.

Yossi Ghinsberg
The adventurer who went over a waterfall (Bolivia, 1981)

Covering more than two million square miles, the Amazon rainforest is an easy place to get lost in. Over the centuries it has claimed the lives of thousands of people who have ventured into its dark and dangerous depths in search of adventure, mysterious tribes and treasure.

At the age of just twenty-two, fresh out of the Israeli navy, Yossi Ghinsberg was desperately keen to explore the area. He joked about discovering a lost tribe, marrying the chieftain's daughter, and finding a fortune in gold and diamonds. Above all, he wanted to experience the romance and adventure he'd read about in books about great explorers. And so, in 1981, he set off into the jungle with three other travellers.

He joked about discovering a lost tribe, marrying the chieftain's daughter, and finding a fortune in gold and diamonds

The three were Karl Rurechter, an Austrian geologist, Marcus Stamm from Switzerland and an American photographer called Kevin Gale. They were not close friends and had met only a short time before beginning their adventure. Very quickly they began experiencing real difficulties, thanks to the exceptionally tough jungle environment and the absence of a professional local guide.

Without proper planning before the expedition set out, the men frequently went hungry too. Fighting their way through thick jungle also sapped their energy even more than they'd expected. The effort soon left all four of them exhausted and fed up.

The wild, overgrown terrain also meant they were making such slow progress that they decided it might make more sense to travel by water. To do this they made a fairly basic raft by lashing together eight massive logs. However, after a series of clashes and disagreements, Rurechter and Stamm decided not to travel on the raft. They quit the expedition there and then and disappeared back into the jungle. Neither was ever seen again.

Though inexperienced, Ghinsberg decided to stick with the raft idea, and together he and Gale began to make their way down the Tuichi River. Everything seemed to be all right to begin with, but then the nature of their journey changed dramatically. The two men found themselves being pitched around violently as the increasingly turbulent waters narrowed to enter the San Pedro Canyon. The ravine was strewn with rocks and debris, and their raft quickly became dangerously unstable in the churning white water. The primitive craft briefly wedged itself beneath the edge of a big boulder and, seizing his opportunity to escape, Gale leaped to safety.

Unfortunately, as he jumped the raft dislodged, and to Ghinsberg's horror it started off downstream towards a deep waterfall. Moments later it went over the edge and he found himself plunged into the depths. Rolled over and over by the force of the falling water, he was literally swallowed by the current.

As he jumped the raft dislodged, and to Ghinsberg's horror it started off downstream towards a deep waterfall

Remarkably, Ghinsberg managed to make it back to the surface before his breath was exhausted, but for the next fifteen minutes he was tossed in every direction as the river made its way further down the canyon. He eventually clambered onto the relative safety of the bank, but there was no sign of the raft, which had presumably been smashed to bits in the tumult.

He had lost his backpack and supplies too. All he had was what was in his pockets: a little food, a first-aid kit and a small torch. Surprisingly, he hadn't broken any bones and could find no cuts or bruises. In other words he had cheated death, but he was a long way from anywhere safe.

With the raft gone Ghinsberg was now forced back into the jungle, like the two companions who had disappeared. Travelling by foot was just as hard and dangerous as before, and he was now on his own. Over the coming days food was a constant worry. Without a knife or machete, he ate only fruit which fell from the tall trees and the occasional egg he found in unguarded birds' nests.

He also knew he was at constant risk of infection. His body acted like a magnet to scores of vicious and venomous creatures, and his skin was often covered in bloodsucking leeches or bored into by egg-laying insects. But Ghinsberg felt he had a vital secret weapon – his firm conviction that he would get through this and come out the other side.

Initially, after going over the waterfall, he'd assumed that he and Gale would find each other and then plot a route out of the jungle together. When this didn't happen it took him a while to realise that they had indeed lost each other. It took several more days to fully appreciate how alone he was. This should have been daunting but instead he found it exciting, the idea that he was experiencing a true-life adventure like the ones he'd read before coming to South America.

Instead of seeing himself as a victim of disaster, Ghinsberg began to think of himself as some kind of hero. He felt he was someone who could overcome adversity, and he was determined to do it. He reasoned that people who live their whole lives in the jungle have knives and guns and make fires to cook with. He had nothing but had nevertheless survived so far, and this gave him hope.

Admittedly, he had good fortune on his side. He'd gained some experience of wilderness living having spent time with Bedouin tribesmen in the Sinai desert. But the rainforest was very different. Besides its amazing variety of horrible insects and leeches, the Amazon is home to many really dangerous animals. These range from ferocious wild boar to jaguars, and from venomous coral snakes to spiders larger than a man's hand and as heavy as a pack of butter. Killing and eating anything was out of the question – even a creature as ordinary as a frog can be deadly in the Amazon. One of the smallest species of frog produces enough poison to kill a dozen people, and just touching its skin can leave a person paralysed.

Even a creature as ordinary as a frog can be deadly in the Amazon

Luckily Ghinsberg managed to avoid being savaged or bitten by any of these natural-born killers or squeezed to death by a hungry anaconda. (In this part of South America these snakes regularly grow to more than fifteen feet in length and can weigh over 200 pounds.) He did run into a jaguar, however, but was able to scare it off using insect-repellent spray from his first-aid kit.

Overcoming the Amazon's top predator would reinforce anyone's heroic self-image, but Ghinsberg's exhilaration was beginning to falter – travelling alone through such dense jungle was so mentally and physically tough. He almost drowned in a sudden flood, and at least twice he came dangerously close to being sucked into the boggy ground. With no one to haul him out, this could easily have proved fatal.

Loneliness can drain even the strongest person's spirit, and along with increasing hunger he struggled to find the will to go on. By the end of his second week he was reduced to skin and bone, and blistered feet meant he was barely making any progress. For a couple of days he had some company – he thought a young girl was walking by his side, although this was almost certainly only in his imagination. Eventually, after nearly three weeks, he collapsed to the ground. It was then he had his final piece of good fortune.

After losing sight of Ghinsberg at the waterfall Gale had gone for help. He recruited a local boatman and set off back along the river in a dugout canoe to look for his companion. Covering such a huge area the search was long and hard, and nearly three weeks after losing contact with Ghinsberg he was ready to call off the rescue mission and go home. With the aid of the skilled river pilot he'd managed to navigate an impressively long way upstream, but now they were looking for a safe place to turn the boat around before heading back.

... both of them stunned by a miracle that had somehow brought them to precisely the same spot

Incredibly, when they finally found a safe spot to manoeuvre the boat it happened to be right by the stretch of bank where Ghinsberg had collapsed. When Gale spotted him he quickly dragged him onto the boat – his life spared, the two adventurers reunited, and both of them stunned by a miracle that had somehow brought them to precisely the same spot within the vastness of the very largest, most impenetrable rainforest on the planet.

EPILOGUE

The men, women and children in this book all share one thing: they have looked death in the face, battled against almost impossible odds and somehow lived to tell the tale. How they did it varies widely, just as their stories all differ enormously.

Many found themselves in danger through accident or bad luck, others by seeking out adventure and excitement, or by looking for new ways to test their abilities and skills. Either way it is impossible not to be awed by their ingenuity and determination, and to marvel at the courage of the people who risked their own lives to mount rescue attempts when all hope seemed lost.

Of course, it's hard for us to imagine how we might cope in these situations. Even people who enjoy taking risks have no idea how they might react if their lives were threatened. This is why one of the best things about true stories like these is seeing how ordinary people can accomplish extraordinary things when disaster strikes.

Crossing jungles and deserts, getting lost in caves and volcanoes, or drifting helplessly in the vast emptiness of the world's largest ocean, everyone in this book found the energy, self-belief and personal resources they needed to survive. Their stories show how it's possible to accomplish the most amazing feats of endurance, strength and stamina, and to do this even when exhausted or seriously injured.

Naturally, no one in this book would want to go through it all again, but it's interesting that many of them said afterwards how much they'd learned from their ordeals. Surviving a disaster can certainly give new meaning to life, and so often those who experience the truly horrifying, find something positive in the end.

DON'T MISS
THESE OTHER INSPIRING
COLLECTIONS . . .

NOT ALL HEROES ARE HUMAN . . .

HEROES

INCREDIBLE TRUE STORIES OF COURAGEOUS ANIMALS

DAVID LONG   KERRY HYNDMAN

YOU DON'T NEED SUPERPOWERS TO BE A REAL-LIFE HERO

RESCUE

DARING MISSIONS FROM ON, UNDER AND ABOVE THE EARTH
From the winners of the Blue Peter Book Award

DAVID LONG   KERRY HYNDMAN